COOKING WITH

Bon Appétit

Peach Pie

Double crust or streusel topping, they're both great!

Crust: Makes 1 crust (double for a two-crust pie)

½	Cup butter (1 stick)
1	Cup all purpose flour
1	TB. sugar
¼	tsp. salt
2-3	TB. milk

Crust topping:

1	egg white
1	tsp. water
2-3	TB. VANILLA SUGAR (for sprinkling on top)

Streusel Topping:

½	Cup cold butter (1 stick)
¾	Cup flour
⅔	Cup sugar
1	tsp. CINNAMON

Filling:

5	Cups sliced ripe peaches (8-10 peaches)
2-3	TB. ARROWROOT STARCH
2-3	TB. cool water
2	tsp. CINNAMON
½	Cup granulated white sugar

Preheat the oven to 375°. To prepare crust, cut butter into bits–it doesn't have to be cold, but it shouldn't be warm to the point of melting. Add dry ingredients, mix by hand to combine, then add milk in a thin stream, using just enough for the dough to hold together. Pat the dough into a circular shape, wrap in plastic wrap and chill while peeling peaches. This makes the dough easier to roll out. If you make two batches for a double crust, divide in half and wrap separately.

If using streusel instead of a top crust, cut cold butter into bits in a small bowl, add the remaining ingredients, and rub between your fingers until a sandy, pebbly consistency is reached. Set aside until needed.

Wash and peel peaches, slice and place in a large bowl with CINNAMON and sugar. In a small bowl, combine ARROWROOT STARCH and water, whisk to blend. Use 3 TB. ARROWROOT and water if the peaches are very juicy, 2 TB. if not. Pour over the peaches and mix gently. Let stand while rolling out crust.

Sprinkle work surface and the top of the dough with flour. Starting from the center, roll out gently to form a circle. Flip the dough once, sprinkle again with flour to keep the dough from sticking. Roll a few inches larger than the pie dish, to allow for the sides. Gently move the crust into the pie plate and pat into place. Add peaches and top with streusel

Chili Powder

There is a difference between chili pepper and chili powder. Chili pepper consists solely of chili pods which have been dried, then powdered. Chili powder is a blend, of which ground chili pepper is used as a base (usually 80% of total volume), with the addition of spices such as cumin and Mexican oregano. For chili, start with 1 TB. (some people will use as much as 3 TB.) per quart.

Regular Chili Powder *SALT FREE*

Rich flavor, deep color, very little heat. This blend is the traditional backbone of many Mexican dishes, from burritos to tamales. Great for family-style chili, use 1-3 TB. per quart. Serve with a shaker jar of crushed hot peppers on the side for those who like heat. *Hand-mixed from: Ancho chili pepper, cumin, garlic, Mexican oregano.*

1/4 cup plastic jar (net 1.2 oz.) #11134 **$2.89**
1/2 cup glass jar (net 2.5 oz.) #11150 **$4.79**
4 oz. bag #11147 **$4.45**
8 oz. bag #11189 **$7.89**
1 lb. bag #11118 **$14.80**

Celery Salt

Celery salt is a wonderful seasoning for beef- perfect for roast beef, pot roast, steaks on the grill, or mixed in meatloaf, 1/2 -1 tsp. per lb., with pepper and garlic. Traditional for sprinkling in tomato juice and what could be better than a Bloody Mary topped with a generous sprinkle of celery salt? *Hand-mixed from: fine salt and celery.*

1/4 cup plastic jar (net 2.3 oz.) #20930 **$2.35**
1/2 cup glass jar (net 4.6 oz.) #20956 **$3.69**
4 oz. bag #20943 **$1.79**
8 oz. bag #20985 **$2.59**
1 lb. bag #20914 **$4.20**

Celery Seed

Black pepper is the best spice for beef, but good cooks also add a touch of celery. Whole celery seed is used in salad dressings, soups and pickling recipes, and rubbed on large cuts of meat. Ground celery is used more sparingly to season smaller, quicker cooking cuts. Use half as much ground celery as whole celery.

Whole Indian Celery Seed
1/4 cup plastic jar (net .9 oz.) #51136 **$2.15**
1/2 cup glass jar (net 1.9 oz.) #51152 **$3.29**
4 oz. bag #51149 **$2.45**
8 oz. bag #51181 **$3.89**
1 lb. bag #51110 **$6.80**

Ground Indian Celery Seed
1/4 cup plastic jar (net .9 oz.) #41133 **$2.29**
1/2 cup glass jar (net 1.9 oz.) #41159 **$3.55**
4 oz. bag #41146 **$2.95**
8 oz. bag #41188 **$4.85**
1 lb. bag #41117 **$8.70**

See FULL INDEX on page 48

COOKING WITH

Bon Appétit

French Country Favorites

THE KNAPP PRESS
Publishers
Los Angeles

Bon Appétit® is a registered trademark of Bon Appétit Publishing Corp. Used with permission.

Copyright © 1987 by Knapp Communications Corporation

Published by The Knapp Press
5900 Wilshire Boulevard, Los Angeles, California 90036

Library of Congress Cataloging-in-Publication Data

French country favorites.

  (Cooking with Bon appétit)
  Includes index.
  1. Cookery, French. I. Bon appétit. II. Series.
TX719.F793 1987   641.5944   87-3100
ISBN 0-89535-181-1

On the cover *(clockwise from top right): Sausages Wrapped in Buckwheat Crepes; Pot-roasted Chicken with Candied Onions and Asparagus; Roasted Loin of Veal with Three Vegetables; Oysters in Cider Vinegar Butter; Brittany Fish Soup. Photo by Jerry Friedman*

Printed and bound in the United States of America

10   9   8   7   6   5   4   3   2   1

❦ Contents

Foreword...................................... *vii*

1 Appetizers and First Courses....... 1

2 Soups and Salads..................... 17
  Soups 18
  Salads 28

3 Eggs and Cheese..................... 37

4 Meat................................. 45
  Beef 46
  Veal 49
  Lamb 53
  Pork 55

5 Poultry and Game.................... 61

6 Fish and Shellfish................... 73

7 Vegetables, Grains and Breads..... 81
  Vegetables 82
  Grains 86
  Breads 87

8 Desserts.................................... 95
    Fruit Desserts 96
    Tarts, Pastries and Confections 100
    Puddings, Soufflés and Ices 105
    Cakes and Tortes 110

Index....................................... 115

❧ *Foreword*

For centuries the *haute cuisine* of France, the refined artistry of its royal kitchens and elegant restaurants, has been extolled and imitated throughout the world as the height of culinary accomplishment. Now, in this collection of recipes, you will be able to explore an even more venerable tradition—the honest and hearty *cuisine bourgeoise,* the solid home cooking of the countryside that is the passion of every Frenchman and the inspiration of many a great French chef.

Country cooking is basically regional cuisine, every province having its distinctive specialties that have evolved over the years out of available ingredients, local character and circumstances—and a French genius for creating delicious and satisfying food from whatever is on hand. One writer calls it "imaginative economy," a sort of peasant thriftiness that is seen throughout the country, such as in the Southwest, where every part of a duck is used, from its plump breasts for *confit* and its liver for stuffings and salads, to its wings and carcass for soup—even its tail feathers are used as a basting brush for pastry. In the prosperous northern region of Normandy, which is famous for, among other things, its apple orchards, you will find this humble fruit used in a wonderful array of foods, from soups and salads to roasted meats and buttery pastries, and to produce the region's legendary cider and Calvados brandy, both of which are used liberally in cooking as well as for drinking.

You will find in this volume representative foods from every part of France, from the sunny Mediterranean hillsides of Provence to the picturesque mountainside towns of Alsace; from the vineyards and fertile river valleys of Champagne to the limestone cliffs and ancient walled villages of the Dordogne; from the bustling open-air markets of the Loire to the rugged coastline of Brittany. Some of the recipes are variations of regional specialties; many are updated versions of classics. Basically, the cooking is simple and straightforward; success depends upon using quality ingredients rather than fancy techniques. What you will also find in this cookbook is the "flavor" of French country cooking—the color, the richness, the passion for good food that is so distinctively French.

1 ❦ Appetizers and First Courses

In the traditional French household, appetizers, or *hors d'oeuvres,* are usually served as a first course, and sometimes as the main course for a light summer supper or luncheon. Often made up of small amounts of leftover vegetables and odds and ends of meat and fish, these dishes are an economical way of using up every bit of what is left after other dishes have been prepared. For special occasions such as holidays and company dinners, appetizers may be served with drinks (usually wine or homemade cider or beer) before the meal.

The most popular appetizers tend to be preserved meats, which are found in enormous variety in *charcuteries* in every town. Each region, each town, has its own particular specialty, such as the *andouillette* of the north, the *boudin* of Lyon, *boudin blanc* of Normandy and the celebrated *saucissons* of Alsace. You'll often find sausages cooked inside pastry or bread, such as our Basil Sausage in Saffron Brioche (page 5).

Pâtés and terrines, another common and very versatile type of appetizer, are well represented in this chapter. They range from the simple Herbed Chicken Pâté with Fresh Tomato and Garlic Sauce (page 13) and an easy Sole and Scallop Pâté with Smoked Salmon and Sorrel (page 9), to an elegant Duck Pâté with Walnuts (page 14) and Burgundian Jambon Persillé (page 12), not really a pâté or terrine but a traditional dish of jellied ham with parsley and herbs served from a terrine.

For a special first course, seafood makes a particularly enticing hot appetizer, such as in Lobster, Oyster and Zucchini Tartlets in Champagne Sauce (page 3), warm Trout Mousse served with Mushroom Sauce (page 10) and simply cooked Oysters in Cider Vinegar Butter (page 6). For a refreshing cold dish, there are also many excellent salad ideas in the next chapter (beginning page 28).

Whether it's hot or cold, a simple spread or an impressive terrine, be sure to serve your appetizer with plenty of crusty bread or thin slices of buttered toast as the French do.

Herbed Goat Cheese Butter

Makes about 1 cup

½ cup (1 stick) unsalted butter, cut into 4 pieces, room temperature
4 ounces soft goat cheese (such as Montrachet), room temperature
¼ cup parsley leaves
2 tablespoons fresh dill or 1 teaspoon dried

2 tablespoons snipped fresh chives
Freshly ground pepper
Crackers, melba toast or thinly sliced French bread

Blend all ingredients except crackers in processor or blender until smooth, stopping once to scrape down sides of work bowl, about 40 seconds. Transfer mixture to 1-cup crock or bowl. Cover and refrigerate at least 2 hours. (*Can be prepared 3 days ahead.*) Soften slightly at room temperature. Serve with crackers.

Marinated Goat Cheese

The longer the cheese marinates, the more flavorful it will be. Serve it with French bread. The leftover marinade can be used as a tangy salad dressing.

6 servings

12 ounces goat cheese (preferably Montrachet), sliced ½ inch thick
1½ cups (about) olive oil
2 tablespoons herbes de Provence* (or other aromatic herb mixture), crumbled

2 medium garlic cloves, crushed
12 peppercorns
2 bay leaves, crumbled
3 small dried red chilies

Arrange cheese in wide-mouthed jar. Cover with olive oil. Add remaining ingredients. Cover tightly; turn jar over several times. Let stand in cool place at least 24 hours before serving. (*Can be stored in cool place up to 10 days; add more oil to jar as necessary to keep cheese completely covered.*)

*Available at specialty foods stores.

Cherry Tomato and Gruyère Tarts

Makes about twelve 4½-inch tarts

Pâte Brisée
1½ cups all purpose flour
¾ cup (1½ sticks) chilled unsalted butter
Pinch of salt
3 to 4 tablespoons cold water

Tomato Gruyère Topping
2 tablespoons (about) Dijon mustard

6 ounces (about) Gruyère cheese, thinly sliced
30 cherry tomatoes (about), sliced ¼ inch thick, drained on paper towels
1 teaspoon dried thyme, crumbled
Salt and freshly ground pepper
3 ounces Gruyère cheese, grated (1 cup)
Olive oil

For pâte brisée: Blend flour, butter and salt in processor using on/off turns until mixture resembles coarse meal, about 10 seconds. Add 3 tablespoons water. Continue processing until dough just comes together; do not form ball (if dough seems dry, add remaining water a little at a time). Turn dough out on lightly floured surface. With heel of hand, push small pieces of dough down onto surface away from you to blend butter and flour thoroughly. Gather into ball;

divide in half. Flatten each into 6-inch disc. Wrap dough in waxed paper. Refrigerate no more than 20 minutes (to prevent butter from hardening).

Roll 1 half out on generously floured surface into 13-inch circle. Cut dough into rounds using 4½-inch cutter. Transfer rounds to rimmed baking sheet. Gather scraps; reroll and cut additional rounds. Repeat with remaining half. Cover and refrigerate.

For topping: Spread thin layer of mustard on each round. Cover with sliced Gruyère. Top with sliced tomatoes. Sprinkle with thyme, salt and pepper. Cover with grated Gruyère, leaving ½-inch border. Drizzle olive oil over. Repeat with remaining rounds.

Preheat oven to 425°F. Bake until pastry is golden brown on bottom, 15 to 20 minutes. Serve immediately.

Lobster, Oyster and Zucchini Tartlets in Champagne Sauce

Shellfish stars in this elegant, lightly sauced appetizer. For a pretty striped effect on the zucchini, use a vegetable peeler to remove strips of peel.

6 servings

Tartlets
- 1½ cups sifted all purpose flour
- ¼ cup finely ground almonds
- 1 teaspoon salt
  Dash of ground cardamom
- 9 tablespoons well-chilled unsalted butter, cut into 9 pieces
- 2 tablespoons ice water

Filling
- 3 quarts water
- 3 medium onions, sliced
- 2 medium leeks, green part only, sliced
- 3 shallots, sliced
- 1 tablespoon mixed white and black peppercorns
- 1 teaspoon salt
  Large bouquet garni (thyme, parsley stems, bay leaf)

- 2 live 1½-pound lobsters
- 2 dozen fresh oysters
- 1 cup French extra-brut or brut Champagne
- 2 shallots, minced
  Small bouquet garni (thyme, parsley stems, bay leaf)
- 10 tablespoons (1¼ sticks) unsalted butter, room temperature
- 2 small zucchini, peeled and very thinly sliced
- 1 tablespoon snipped fresh chives
- 1 tablespoon thinly sliced green onion

For tartlets: Mix flour, almonds, salt and cardamom in processor 30 seconds. Cut in butter using on/off turns until mixture resembles coarse meal. With machine running, add water through feed tube and blend just until dough comes together; do not form ball. Flatten into disc. Wrap in plastic and refrigerate at least 1 hour.

Preheat oven to 425°F. Roll dough out on lightly floured surface to thickness of 1/16 inch. Cut out six 4- to 5-inch circles. Fit into six 3½-inch tartlet pans with removable bottoms. Trim edges. Pierce bottoms with fork. Line with parchment paper or foil and fill with dried beans or pie weights. Bake until pastry is set, about 10 minutes. Remove paper and beans and continue baking pastry until brown, about 5 minutes. Set aside.

For filling: Combine water, onions, leeks, 3 shallots, peppercorns, salt and large bouquet garni in bottom of steamer and bring to boil. Reduce heat and simmer 20 minutes.

Arrange lobsters on rack and place in steamer. Cover and steam 8 to 10 minutes. Strain liquid and reserve. Shell lobsters. Slice tail meat ⅓ inch thick; halve claw meat lengthwise. Wrap in plastic. Reserve small lobster legs and 1⅓ teaspoons roe (if available).

Shuck oysters. Place in fine strainer over bowl and drain 1 hour.

Carefully remove "scallop" (adductor muscle) from each oyster; do not tear oyster. Place scallops in heavy medium saucepan; set oysters aside.

Add drained oyster liquor, ½ cup reserved lobster cooking liquid, Champagne, 2 shallots and small bouquet garni to oyster scallops. Cook over medium-low heat until reduced to ⅔ cup.

Crush reserved small lobster legs. Transfer to heavy small saucepan. Add 4 tablespoons butter. Cook over medium-low heat until butter melts. Cover and let stand at room temperature until butter is orange and tastes strongly of lobster, about 1 hour.

Melt 1 tablespoon butter in heavy large skillet over medium heat. Add zucchini and sauté 1 minute. Add oysters and sear quickly on both sides. Mix in sliced lobster meat.

Preheat oven to 375°F. Reheat tartlets. Bring Champagne reduction to boil. Quickly whisk in remaining 5 tablespoons butter all at once. Remove from heat and whisk in melted lobster butter. Strain into zucchini mixture. Crumble roe and add to mixture. Spoon into tartlets. Sprinkle with chives and onion and serve immediately.

Snails in Puff Pastry Shells

Hazelnuts give this favorite a new twist. A great party starter.

Makes 3 dozen

3 dozen snails, undrained
½ cup Chardonnay or dry white wine
1 medium onion, minced
1 shallot, minced
2 garlic cloves, minced
  Salt and freshly ground pepper
  Freshly grated nutmeg

1 pound puff pastry, preferably homemade

1 egg yolk blended with 3 tablespoons milk (glaze)

¾ cup (1½ sticks) well-chilled unsalted butter, cut into 12 pieces
⅓ cup chopped toasted hazelnuts
3 tablespoons minced fresh parsley

Drain snail juices into small saucepan. Place snails in bowl. Add wine, onion, shallot, garlic, salt, pepper and nutmeg to juices and bring to boil. Pour marinade over snails. Let cool. Cover and refrigerate for 24 hours.

Preheat oven to 425°F. Butter baking sheets. Roll dough out on lightly floured surface to thickness of ¼ inch. Cut out 36 circles using 2-inch floured cutter. Arrange circles on prepared sheets. Using knife tip, trace lid on each circle ¾ inch in from edge; do not cut through dough. Brush with glaze. Bake pastry until puffed and golden brown, about 10 minutes. Cool slightly on rack. Using sharp knife, cut out lids. Discard any soft dough inside shells. Reduce oven temperature to 375°F.

Strain marinade into large saucepan, pressing down on vegetables to extract all liquid. Boil until reduced to ½ cup. Remove pan from heat and whisk in 2 pieces of butter. Set pan over low heat and whisk in remaining butter 1 piece at a time. Mix in snails, hazelnuts and parsley. Adjust seasoning. Place 1 snail and some of sauce inside each shell. Top with lid. Bake until heated through.

Basil Sausage in Saffron Brioche

Making the sausage a few days ahead allows the flavors to mellow. Excellent served with robust Tomato Mustard.

12 servings

Basil Sausage
- ¹/₂ pound pork fatback
- ¹/₂ pound boneless veal top round
- ¹/₄ pound boneless pork shoulder
- ¹/₄ pound boneless pork loin
- ¹/₂ cup thinly sliced fresh basil
- ¹/₄ cup Cognac
- 2 teaspoons pureed garlic
- 1³/₄ teaspoons salt
- 1 teaspoon freshly ground pepper
- ¹/₂ teaspoon ground allspice
- ¹/₂ teaspoon freshly grated nutmeg
- 2 to 4 eggs

- 10 cups (about) chicken broth

Saffron Brioche
- 2 tablespoons warm milk (105°F to 115°F)
- 1 tablespoon warm water (105°F to 115°F)

- 1 tablespoon sugar
- 2 teaspoons saffron threads, crumbled
- ¹/₂ envelope dry yeast

- 2¹/₄ cups (about) all purpose flour
- 1 teaspoon salt
- 3 eggs, room temperature
- 1 cup (2 sticks) unsalted butter, room temperature

- 1 egg white, beaten to blend
- 1 egg yolk mixed with 2 tablespoons milk (glaze)

Tomato Mustard*

For sausage: Grind first 4 ingredients through coarse blade of meat grinder. Grind half of mixture again through fine blade. Combine both meat mixtures with basil, Cognac, garlic, salt, pepper, allspice, nutmeg and 2 eggs. Blend in 1 or 2 more eggs if necessary to make sausage that is moist but not too loose. To check seasoning, pinch off small piece of mixture and fry until cooked through. Taste, then adjust seasonings of uncooked portion.

Cut 16 × 25-inch piece of cheesecloth. Form meat into 10-inch-long cylinder in center of cheesecloth. Wrap cheesecloth around sausage, twisting ends in opposite directions; tie with string.

Pour enough chicken broth into fish poacher or large pot to cover sausage. Bring to simmer. Add sausage. Cover and simmer gently until juices run clear when pierced, turning sausage frequently, about 40 minutes. Cool in poaching liquid 15 minutes. Drain and cool completely. (*Can be prepared 3 days ahead. Cover and refrigerate.*)

For brioche: Combine milk, water, sugar and saffron in bowl of heavy-duty electric mixer. Sprinkle yeast over liquid; stir to dissolve. Let stand until foamy, about 10 minutes.

Add 1¹/₄ cups flour and salt to yeast and beat 3 minutes on low speed. Beat in eggs 1 at a time. Add 1 cup flour and beat until dough is light and silky. Add butter in 4 additions. Beat until dough is elastic, about 4 minutes. Transfer dough to well-floured surface. Lift with floured hand and slap against surface about 6 times, until soft and slightly sticky dough forms, using pastry scraper as aid. Transfer to large bowl. Cover bowl and let dough rise in warm draft-free area until doubled in volume, about 1¹/₂ hours.

Punch dough down with floured hand. Cover and refrigerate until firm, at least 40 minutes.

Preheat oven to 350°F. Butter large baking sheet. Punch dough down with floured hand. Roll dough out on well-floured surface to 8 × 12-inch rectangle.

Remove cheesecloth from sausage. Brush sausage with egg white. Place lengthwise in center of dough. Wrap dough tightly around sausage, folding in ends and brushing with glaze to seal. Brush dough lightly with glaze. Pierce several times with tines of fork. Arrange seam side down in prepared pan. Bake until golden brown, about 30 minutes. Cool on rack. (*Can be prepared 1 day ahead. Cover and refrigerate.*) Serve sausage warm or at room temperature. Pass mustard separately.

*Tomato Mustard

Makes about 1¹/₃ cups

14 oil-cured olives, pitted
1 cup Dijon mustard

¹/₂ cup finely diced sun-dried
 tomatoes
1 garlic clove, pureed

Finely mince olives, then mash to puree with side of knife or in mortar with pestle. Measure 2 tablespoons. Transfer to bowl. Mix in remaining ingredients. (*Mustard can be prepared up to 1 week ahead and refrigerated.*)

Steamed Clams in Wine Broth

2 servings

6 tablespoons (³/₄ stick) unsalted
 butter, melted
¹/₄ cup dry white wine
¹/₄ cup water
1 tablespoon minced fresh parsley

Dash of hot pepper sauce
1¹/₂ pounds fresh clams, scrubbed

Lemon wedges

Bring 2 tablespoons butter, wine, water, parsley and hot pepper sauce to boil in bottom of steamer. Arrange clams on rack and place in steamer. Cover; steam until clams open, 6 to 10 minutes. Discard any that do not open.

 Divide clams in their shells between 2 shallow bowls. Strain broth; ladle over clams. Divide remaining 4 tablespoons melted butter between 2 small dishes for dipping. Garnish with lemon wedges and serve immediately.

Oysters in Cider Vinegar Butter

Makes 36

36 unshucked oysters, scrubbed

¹/₂ cup hard cider (preferably
 imported)
¹/₃ cup clam juice
2 tablespoons cider vinegar
4 medium shallots, minced
1 leek (white part only), minced

³/₄ cup (1¹/₂ sticks) well-chilled
 unsalted butter, cut into ¹/₂-inch
 pieces
¹/₂ cup whipping cream
 Salt and freshly ground pepper

Coarse salt
2 tablespoons snipped fresh chives

Open oysters, reserving liquor and deep halves of shells. Transfer oysters to small bowl. Scrape inside of shells very well over nonaluminum saucepan. Transfer shells to large pot. Cover with generously salted hot water.

 Add reserved oyster liquor, cider, clam juice, vinegar, shallots and leek to saucepan with oyster scrapings. Simmer over medium heat until reduced to

½ cup (liquid and solids combined), about 6 minutes. Increase heat to high and bring to vigorous boil. Immediately whisk in butter, 1 piece at a time. Strain sauce through fine sieve into clean pan. Simmer cream in heavy small pan until reduced to ¼ cup, about 3 minutes. Add to sauce. Season with salt and pepper.

Place pot with oyster shells over medium heat to warm shells. Cover jelly roll pan with ¼ inch coarse salt. Preheat broiler. Remove warm shells from water and dry. Spoon ½ teaspoon sauce into each shell. Add 1 oyster to each and cover with remaining sauce. Set filled shells on prepared pan. Broil 4 inches from heat until sauce is golden, watching carefully. Sprinkle with chives and serve immediately.

Baked Oysters with Rouille

6 servings

Coarse salt
36 to 48 oysters, well scrubbed

Rouille*

Preheat oven to 450°F. Cover baking sheet with ½-inch layer coarse salt. Heat in oven 5 minutes. Arrange oysters flat side up atop salt. Bake until shells begin to open, about 10 minutes. Finish opening oysters with knife, protecting hand with cloth and discarding upper shells. Place ½ teaspoon Rouille atop each and serve immediately.

*Rouille

Makes about 1 cup

½ **cup parsley leaves**
1½ **slices firm white bread, crusts trimmed, cut into 1-inch pieces**
4 **large garlic cloves**
1 **4-ounce jar pimientos (undrained)**
1 **teaspoon dried red pepper flakes**

½ **teaspoon dried basil, crumbled**
½ **teaspoon salt**
¼ **teaspoon cayenne pepper**
⅓ **cup olive oil (preferably extra virgin)**

Place parsley and bread in processor work bowl. With machine running, drop garlic through feed tube and mince finely. Add pimientos with liquid, red pepper flakes, basil, salt and cayenne. Puree until smooth, about 15 seconds. With machine running, slowly pour oil through feed tube and blend 5 seconds. (*Can be refrigerated 2 weeks. Bring to room temperature before serving.*)

Tiger Prawns Provençal

4 servings

Tomato Concassée
1 **tablespoon olive oil**
1 **medium shallot, minced**
2 **medium garlic cloves, minced**
2 **pounds tomatoes, peeled and diced**
1 **tablespoon minced fresh basil**
1 **teaspoon freshly ground pepper**
1 **bay leaf**

Prawns
8 **uncooked tiger prawns, shelled (except for tail) and deveined**

1 **tablespoon olive oil**
2 **medium garlic cloves, minced**
¼ **cup dry white wine**

8 **asparagus tips, blanched**
4 **yellow tomato baskets**
Radicchio leaves
Italian parsley leaves
Chopped Italian parsley

For concassée: Heat oil in heavy large skillet over medium heat. Add shallot and garlic and stir until translucent, about 2 minutes. Add tomatoes, basil, pepper and bay leaf. Cover and simmer 5 minutes. Uncover and simmer until very thick and no liquid remains, stirring occasionally, about 30 minutes. (*Can be prepared 3 days ahead. Cool completely, cover and refrigerate.*)

For prawns: To butterfly prawns, slice ³/₄ way through rounded side to ¹/₄ inch from tail. Open prawns, flattening gently; rinse if necessary. Heat oil in heavy large skillet over medium heat. Add garlic and cook until sizzling. Remove skillet from heat. Arrange prawns skin side down in single layer in skillet, pressing gently. Pull tail pieces apart so prawns lie flat. Return skillet to heat and cook prawns 1 minute. Reduce heat to medium. Cover and cook until prawns are just opaque, 3 to 4 minutes. Remove prawns from skillet; tent with foil to keep warm. Add wine to skillet and boil until reduced by half. Add concassée and simmer until thickened.

Place 2 asparagus tips in each tomato basket. Spoon concassée on platter. Arrange prawns skin side up on concassée. Pull up tail. Garnish with tomato baskets, radicchio and parsley.

Brandade of Salt Cod on Garlic Croutons

The word brandade *derives from the French verb* brandir *meaning "to brandish with a cane," and refers to the traditional method of pounding the cod with a mortar and pestle.*

4 to 6 servings

2 pounds salt cod

Garlic Croutons
12 ¹/₄- to ¹/₂-inch-thick slices French bread
   Olive oil
2 garlic cloves, halved

2 large garlic cloves, crushed
¹/₂ cup hot milk

¹/₂ cup hot whipping cream
1 cup olive oil
   Fresh lemon juice
   Pinch of freshly grated nutmeg
   Salt and freshly ground pepper

   Niçoise olives and parsley sprigs

Cover salt cod with cold water and refrigerate 24 hours, changing water 8 times to remove all salt.

For croutons: Position rack in center of oven and preheat to 400°F. Arrange bread slices in single layer on baking sheet. Brush tops with oil. Bake until just beginning to color, 5 minutes. Rub both sides with cut edges of garlic.

Drain cod; cover with cold water in large saucepan and bring just to simmer. Let simmer gently until cod is tender and just begins to flake, 8 to 10 minutes. Drain cod; break into small pieces. Transfer to processor. Add 2 crushed garlic cloves. Combine hot milk and cream. With machine running, pour olive oil and milk mixture alternately through feed tube, several tablespoons at a time, and blend until smooth. Season brandade with lemon juice, nutmeg, salt and pepper.

Mound brandade in center of platter. Surround with croutons, olives and parsley. Serve at room temperature. (*Can be prepared 3 days ahead.*)

Sole and Scallop Pâté with Smoked Salmon and Sorrel

6 to 8 servings

Sole and Scallop Puree
- ³/₄ pound fillet of sole, cut into small pieces
- ³/₄ pound scallops
- 2 egg whites
- ³/₄ cup whipping cream
- 1¹/₂ teaspoons salt
- Freshly ground pepper
- Pinch of cayenne pepper

Smoked Salmon Puree
- ¹/₄ pound lightly smoked salmon
- ¹/₃ cup whipping cream
- 1 teaspoon minced fresh mint

Sorrel Mixture
- 2 tablespoons (¹/₄ stick) butter
- 6 ounces stemmed sorrel leaves, deveined and coarsely chopped
- 2 egg yolks
- 2 tablespoons whipping cream

Thinly sliced smoked salmon (optional)
Beurre Blanc*

For sole and scallops: Freeze bowl of heavy-duty mixer until very cold. Puree sole and scallops in processor until smooth. Press firmly through fine sieve a little at a time, scraping mixture from bottom of sieve into chilled mixer bowl. Transfer to mixer fitted with flat paddle. Gradually blend in whites at medium speed, then cream. Season with salt and peppers. Cover and refrigerate until ready to use.

For salmon: Puree salmon, cream and mint in food mill fitted with fine blade (do not use food processor).

For sorrel: Melt 2 tablespoons butter in heavy large saucepan over medium-high heat. Add sorrel and stir until wilted. Drain. Transfer to bowl. Mix in yolks, cream and pinch of salt.

Preheat oven to 350°F. Butter 4-cup loaf pan. Spread half of sole and scallop puree in bottom and up sides of pan. Cover with all of sorrel mixture. Top with half of remaining sole puree. Cover with all of salmon puree. Finish with remaining sole puree. Cover with buttered parchment. (*Can be prepared 6 to 8 hours ahead to this point, covered and refrigerated.*) Set pan in larger pan. Add enough simmering water to come halfway up sides of pan. Bake until top is springy to touch, about 35 minutes.

Run tip of sharp knife around edge of pâté and invert onto platter. Arrange salmon crosswise over top if desired. Slice thinly. Serve with Beurre Blanc.

*Beurre Blanc

Makes about 1 cup

- 6 tablespoons water
- 4 tablespoons tarragon wine vinegar
- 3 tablespoons minced green onion (white part only)
- 1 cup (2 sticks) unsalted butter, cut into 16 pieces, well chilled
- 1 teaspoon salt
- Freshly ground white pepper

Combine water, vinegar and onion in heavy small saucepan. Set in slightly larger saucepan of gently simmering water over low heat and boil until mixture is reduced to 3 tablespoons, about 20 minutes. Whisk in butter 1 tablespoon at a time, completely incorporating each before adding next and adjusting heat as necessary so bottom of pan is never too hot to touch. If sauce breaks down at any time, remove from water bath and whisk in cold piece of butter. Season sauce with salt and pepper.

Trout Mousse with Mushroom Sauce

6 servings

Trout Mousse

1¼ pounds fresh trout fillets,*
   skinned and boned (about
   2½ pounds before skinning
   and boning)
 1 egg
 1 egg white
⅓ cup half and half
   Pinch of freshly grated nutmeg

½ cup (1 stick) unsalted butter,
   room temperature
¼ teaspoon freshly grated nutmeg
   Salt and freshly ground white
   pepper
 2 to 3 cups whipping cream

 2 tablespoons (¼ stick) butter

Mushroom Sauce

 1 tablespoon unsalted butter
 1 pound button mushrooms

½ cup fish stock or clam juice
½ cup dry white wine
 1 medium onion, finely chopped
 2 medium shallots, finely chopped
 2 garlic cloves, mashed
 1 ½ × 1½-inch lemon peel strip
   Bouquet garni (parsley, thyme, bay
   leaf)
½ cup (1 stick) unsalted butter, cut
   into tablespoon-size pieces
 2 tablespoons minced fresh parsley
⅓ teaspoon saffron threads, crushed
   Fresh lemon juice

   Lemon slices
   Italian parsley bouquets

For mousse: Remove oily brown tissue from skin side of each trout fillet. Weigh remaining white meat; you should have between 16 and 17 ounces. Cut into 1-inch cubes. Puree in processor with egg, egg white, half and half and nutmeg until smooth, scraping down sides of bowl. Press through fine sieve a little at a time, pushing hard with heavy wooden pestle or plastic pastry scraper. Scrape mixture from bottom of sieve into metal bowl. Set bowl in larger bowl filled with ice. Cover with plastic wrap and refrigerate 2 hours. Wash and dry processor bowl; refrigerate 2 hours.

Transfer fish puree to processor. Add ½ cup butter, nutmeg, salt and pepper and mix until smooth and homogenous, about 2 minutes, scraping down sides and up bottom of bowl. Add 2 cups whipping cream through feed tube in slow steady stream, scraping down sides of bowl. Poach 1 tablespoon mixture in small amount of barely simmering salted water 4 minutes. If texture is firm and free of fibers, mousse is ready. If not, blend in up to 1 cup additional whipping cream in 3 batches, testing mousse for desired texture after each addition.

Preheat oven to 325°F. Butter six 6-ounce ramekins with 2 tablespoons butter. Divide mousse evenly among ramekins. Tap sharply on counter to eliminate air pockets. Cover with parchment. (*Can be prepared 24 hours ahead to this point, covered and refrigerated.*) Arrange ramekins in shallow roasting pan. Add enough simmering water to come halfway up sides of molds. Bake until parchment lifts easily from mousse, about 15 minutes.

For sauce: Melt 1 tablespoon butter in heavy large skillet over medium heat. Stir in mushrooms; season with salt and pepper. Cover and cook until all moisture is rendered, about 4 minutes. Strain liquid into small bowl. Increase heat to high and toss mushrooms to dry. Transfer to another bowl.

Boil reserved mushroom liquid, fish stock, wine, onion, shallots, garlic, lemon peel and bouquet garni in heavy medium saucepan until reduced to ⅓ cup.

Remove from heat and whisk in 1 tablespoon butter. Place over low heat and whisk in remaining butter 1 tablespoon at a time, incorporating each before adding next. If thickened sauce breaks down at any time, remove from heat and whisk in 2 tablespoons cold butter. Strain sauce into clean saucepan. Blend in mushrooms, parsley and saffron. Season sauce to taste with fresh lemon juice and salt and pepper.

Run tip of sharp knife around edge of mousse and invert onto plates. Spoon some of sauce over. Garnish with lemon slices and parsley and serve.

*Use freshwater trout only, not sea trout.

Leek and Ham Timbales

6 servings

1 large garlic clove

2 small leeks, white part only, halved lengthwise and cleaned

2 tablespoons olive oil

3 ounces imported smoked ham, cut into 1/4-inch dice

3 egg whites

2 teaspoons distilled white vinegar

4 egg yolks

1/2 cup whipping cream

3/4 teaspoon minced fresh tarragon or 1/4 teaspoon dried, crumbled

1/4 teaspoon salt
Freshly ground pepper

1/4 cup pine nuts (1 ounce), toasted

1 small tomato, peeled, seeded and quartered

1/4 teaspoon minced fresh tarragon
Pinch of sugar

6 tarragon sprigs

Position rack in center of oven and preheat to 350°F. Butter six 1/3-cup timbale molds or custard cups.

Insert steel knife in processor. With machine running, drop garlic through feed tube and mince finely. Carefully remove steel knife and insert medium slicer.

Stand leeks in feed tube and slice, using medium pressure. Heat oil in heavy 10-inch skillet over low heat. Add garlic, leeks and ham and cook until leeks soften, stirring frequently, about 20 minutes. Set aside. Clean and dry work bowl.

Insert steel knife. Blend whites in work bowl 15 seconds. With machine running, drizzle vinegar through feed tube and process until whites hold shape, about 1 minute. Gently transfer to bowl. Blend yolks, cream, 3/4 teaspoon tarragon, salt and pepper in processor 3 seconds. Add pine nuts and ham mixture and blend using 2 on/off turns. Spoon whites over; blend using 2 on/off turns.

Divide mixture evenly among prepared timbales. Set timbales in large baking dish and place on oven rack. Pour boiling water into baking dish to come halfway up sides of timbales. Bake until tester inserted in centers comes out clean, about 20 minutes. Remove timbales from water bath and let stand 5 minutes. (*Can be prepared 2 days ahead. Cool completely in molds. Cover and refrigerate. Reheat in water bath on top of stove 25 to 30 minutes.*)

Coarsely chop tomato in processor using 2 on/off turns. Add 1/4 teaspoon tarragon, sugar, salt and pepper. Mix using 2 on/off turns. Just before serving, invert warm timbales onto plates. Top each with some of tomato mixture and garnish with tarragon sprig.

Jambon Persillé

In Burgundy this lovely aspic is served directly from the bowl, but it can also be unmolded onto a platter.

6 to 8 servings

1½ pounds Black Forest or Westphalian ham
¼ pound prosciutto, cut into slivers
½ cup minced fresh parsley mixed with ½ cup minced fresh basil, tarragon or dill (or 1 cup minced fresh parsley mixed with 1 tablespoon dried basil, tarragon or dillweed, crumbled)

2 large garlic cloves, minced
3½ cups homemade chicken stock or Quick Chicken Stock*
2 envelopes unflavored gelatin softened in ½ cup cold water

Parsley sprigs and cherry tomatoes
Mustard Mayonnaise**

Combine ham, prosciutto, parsley mixture and garlic. Pack into bottom of 8-cup bowl or soufflé dish (metal bowl works best if unmolding).

Heat stock in medium saucepan over low heat. Add softened gelatin and stir until completely dissolved, about 4 minutes. Pour into another bowl. Set into larger bowl filled with cracked ice and stir frequently until syrupy, about 10 minutes. Pour stock over ham mixture. Tap mold on table to prevent air pockets. Chill until gelatin is set, at least 6 hours or overnight.

To unmold, invert bowl with aspic on serving platter. Wrap bowl with towel soaked in very hot water until aspic is released. Garnish platter with parsley sprigs and cherry tomatoes. Pass Mustard Mayonnaise separately. (For decoration, fan thinly sliced ham over top of mold before pouring in stock.)

*Quick Chicken Stock

Makes about 1 quart

2 14-ounce cans chicken broth
½ cup dry vermouth
4 large garlic cloves, halved
2 tablespoons finely chopped onion

1 bay leaf
1 fresh parsley sprig
¼ teaspoon dried thyme, crumbled

Simmer all ingredients in saucepan 30 minutes. Strain before using.

**Mustard Mayonnaise

Makes 1¼ cups

2 egg yolks, room temperature
1 tablespoon fresh lemon juice or to taste
1 tablespoon Dijon mustard or to taste

Salt and freshly ground pepper
1 to 1¼ cups oil (mixture of half olive oil and half vegetable oil)

Blend yolks, lemon juice, mustard, salt, pepper and 1 tablespoon oil in processor until slightly thickened. With machine running, slowly pour enough remaining oil through feed tube to form thick sauce.

Herbed Chicken Pâté

This marbled pâté is accented by a colorful fresh tomato sauce.

8 servings

2 pounds skinned and boned chicken breast, cut into 1/2-inch pieces

3/4 cup (1 1/2 sticks) unsalted butter
2/3 cup thinly sliced leek (white part only)
1/4 cup thinly sliced shallot

3 egg whites

1 1/2 teaspoons salt
1/4 teaspoon freshly ground pepper

1/8 teaspoon freshly grated nutmeg
2 1/4 cups well-chilled whipping cream

1/2 cup chicken broth
2 cups tightly packed spinach leaves
2 cups tightly packed fresh basil leaves
3/4 cup well-chilled whipping cream

Fresh Tomato and Garlic Sauce*

Puree chicken in processor in 2 batches to very smooth paste. Refrigerate until well chilled, at least 1 hour.

Meanwhile, melt butter in heavy small skillet over low heat. Add leek and shallot and cook until soft, stirring occasionally, about 15 minutes. Cool.

Combine half of chicken with half of leek mixture in processor. Puree until smooth. Add half of egg whites and process until smooth. Transfer to bowl. Repeat with remaining chicken, leek mixture and egg whites. Refrigerate until mixture is well chilled.

Blend half of chicken mixture, salt, pepper and nutmeg in processor. With machine running, slowly pour 1 cup plus 2 tablespoons cream through feed tube. Blend 1 minute. Transfer to large bowl. Repeat with remaining chicken, salt, pepper, nutmeg and 1 cup plus 2 tablespoons cream. Combine both mixtures.

Bring chicken broth to boil in large skillet. Add spinach and basil and toss until just wilted, about 45 seconds. Drain well. Squeeze out any remaining liquid. Puree spinach mixture with remaining 3/4 cup cream until smooth. Blend in 1/4 of chicken mixture.

Preheat oven to 350°F. Line 9 × 5-inch loaf pan with plastic wrap, leaving 5-inch overhang. Pour half of white chicken mixture into pan. Cover with half of spinach mixture. Using knife, swirl through layers to create marble effect. Repeat with remaining chicken and spinach. Tap pan on work surface to settle pâté. Fold overlapping plastic over top of pâté. Cover pan tightly with foil. Place loaf pan in deep roasting pan. Pour enough water into roasting pan to come 2/3 up sides of loaf pan. Transfer to oven and bake 1 1/4 hours. Cool. Weight pâté with heavy object and refrigerate overnight.

Unmold pâté onto platter. Let stand at room temperature 1 hour before serving. Pass tomato sauce separately.

*Fresh Tomato and Garlic Sauce

Makes about 1 1/2 cups

3 1/2 pounds tomatoes, peeled, seeded and chopped
1/4 cup thick salsa
4 garlic cloves, minced

1/2 teaspoon julienne of lemon peel (yellow part only)
Salt and freshly ground pepper
2 tablespoons olive oil

Combine all ingredients except oil in medium bowl. Refrigerate 1 hour. Just before serving, drain off liquid from sauce. Stir in olive oil.

Veal Terrine

Make this three days before serving for best flavor.

14 servings

1 8-ounce ham steak, cut into ½-inch-wide strips
½ cup dry vermouth

2 tablespoons (¼ stick) unsalted butter
1 pound chicken livers, patted dry
¼ cup Cognac
½ cup beef broth
10 juniper berries
1½ bay leaves
2 eggs, beaten to blend
4 shallots, chopped
3 garlic cloves, chopped

1 tablespoon green peppercorns in brine, drained, 1 teaspoon liquid reserved
1½ teaspoons dried thyme, crumbled
1 teaspoon salt
½ teaspoon freshly grated nutmeg
¼ teaspoon freshly ground pepper
¼ teaspoon cinnamon
1 pound coarsely ground veal, room temperature
1 pound coarsely ground pork loin or leg, room temperature

1 pound thinly sliced bacon

Combine ham and vermouth in bowl. Let stand for 1 hour.

Melt butter in heavy large skillet over medium-high heat. Add livers and stir until brown on outside but still pink in center, about 3 minutes. Transfer to processor and cool. Add Cognac to skillet, let heat, then ignite with match. When flames subside, add broth and boil until reduced by half, scraping up any browned bits, about 2 minutes. Grind juniper berries and bay leaves in spice grinder or in mortar with pestle. Add to livers. Add eggs, shallots, garlic, green peppercorns with reserved liquid, thyme, salt, nutmeg, pepper and cinnamon. Process 15 seconds. Transfer to bowl. Add veal and pork. Drain vermouth from ham into mixture; add pan juices. Mix well.

Position rack in center of oven and preheat to 300°F. Line 6-cup enameled or glass terrine with bacon, allowing some to drape over sides. Spread ⅓ of meat mixture in pan. Arrange half of ham over. Add another ⅓ of meat, then remaining ham. Spread remaining meat over. Fold bacon in, covering meat. Cover with foil. Place terrine in large roasting pan. Add enough hot water to roasting pan to come 2 inches up sides of terrine. Bake until thermometer inserted in center registers 180°F, about 3 hours. Remove from oven. Cover with weights and let cool. Remove weights; refrigerate terrine for 3 days. Remove terrine from pan. Serve at room temperature.

Duck Pâté with Walnuts

10 to 12 servings

1 4- to 5-pound duck, liver trimmed, chopped and reserved
Salt and freshly ground pepper
13 tablespoons Cognac

1 pound ground veal
1 pound ground pork
¾ pound pork fat, ground
3 eggs
4 garlic cloves, minced
2 tablespoons green peppercorns, drained and rinsed
3¼ teaspoons salt
1½ teaspoons freshly ground pepper

1 teaspoon ground allspice
1 teaspoon freshly grated nutmeg
1 teaspoon dried thyme, crumbled
½ teaspoon ground cloves
¼ teaspoon dried sage, crumbled
1 cup chopped walnuts

1¼ cups all purpose flour
¾ cup water

Red leaf lettuce
8 cornichons, cut into fans
Toast rounds
Butter roses

Cut wing tips off duck. Using sharp knife, cut along backbone to separate skin from meat. Using fingers, gently remove skin from duck (except for neck flap), using knife when necessary; do not tear skin. Sprinkle skin with salt and pepper. Rub inside of skin with 1 tablespoon Cognac. Wrap in plastic and chill until ready to use.

Separate leg pieces from body. Cut out wishbone, then remove breasts. Separate fillets from breasts and set aside. Cut each breast into 3 strips. Sprinkle with salt and pepper. Transfer to nonaluminum bowl. Add 4 tablespoons Cognac and toss well. Let mixture stand until ready to use.

Bone leg pieces. Remove tendons from meat. Finely grind fillets and duck leg meat in processor using on/off turns. Transfer to large bowl. Add duck liver, remaining 8 tablespoons Cognac, veal, pork, pork fat, eggs, garlic, peppercorns, salt, pepper, allspice, nutmeg, thyme, cloves and sage and mix well. Fry small patty of mixture. Taste; adjust seasoning of uncooked mixture. Stir in walnuts.

Preheat oven to 350°F. Line 2- to 2½-quart terrine mold with duck skin. Spoon half of mixture into prepared mold, patting firmly to pack tightly. Top with duck breast strips. Cover with remaining mixture, packing tightly. Fold skin over. Top with terrine lid. Whisk flour and water until smooth. Apply over juncture of lid and mold to seal completely. (Or cover terrine tightly with foil.) Set mold in roasting pan. Add enough water to pan to come halfway up sides of mold. Bring to boil. Transfer to oven and bake until tester inserted halfway into pâté for 30 seconds comes out hot and juices run clear, about 2½ hours.

Remove pâté from water bath. Take off lid. Cover top of pâté with heavy-duty foil. Top foil with 2-pound weight. Let pâté stand until cool. Refrigerate at least 3 days.

Line plates with lettuce. Cut pâté into thin slices, then halve crosswise. Set one half on each plate. Top with cornichon. Serve with toast and butter.

Chef's Game Terrine

Any type of game animal or bird can be used: Try venison, rabbit, partridge or pheasant. Make the terrine at least three days in advance so flavors can mellow.

10 to 12 servings

1 tablespoon butter
1 pound skinned and boned game meat, cut into ¼-inch dice, bones reserved and cracked into large pieces*
2 shallots, minced
3 tablespoons Cognac
3 tablespoons Madeira
1 cup veal or beef stock
3 tablespoons dry white wine

4 ounces chicken livers, cut into ¼-inch dice
4 ounces cooked ham, cut into ¼-inch dice
4 ounces pork fat, cut into ¼-inch dice
3 tablespoons peeled pistachios
2 teaspoons salt
1 teaspoon ground allspice

1 teaspoon freshly ground pepper
1 ½-ounce can truffle pieces with juice (optional)

2 tablespoons (¼ stick) butter
4 ounces chicken livers
4 ounces mushrooms, finely chopped
3 tablespoons Cognac
3 tablespoons Madeira
8 ounces pork fat
4 ounces lean pork
4 ounces lean veal

8 ounces bacon
1 fresh thyme sprig
1 bay leaf

Melt butter in heavy large skillet over medium heat. Add bones and brown on all sides. Add shallots and stir 3 minutes. Pour Cognac and Madeira into corner of skillet; heat and ignite. When flames subside, pour in stock and wine. Bring to boil, stirring up browned bits. Boil until liquid is reduced to ½ cup. Strain liquid and cool.

Mix reduced liquid, game, livers, ham, fat, pistachios, salt, allspice, pepper and truffle with juice (if desired) in large nonaluminum bowl. Cover and let stand at room temperature 2 hours, or refrigerate overnight.

Melt 1 tablespoon butter in heavy large skillet over medium-high heat. Add chicken livers and sauté until just firm and pink inside, 2 to 3 minutes. Remove from skillet. Melt remaining 1 tablespoon butter in same skillet over medium heat. Add mushrooms and cook until all liquid evaporates, stirring occasionally, about 5 minutes. Return livers to skillet. Add Cognac and Madeira and simmer until alcohol evaporates, about 2 minutes. Grind liver mixture, fat, pork and veal through fine plate of meat grinder into large bowl. Add game mixture. Beat with wooden spoon until mixture clings together and pulls away from sides of bowl, 2 to 3 minutes. Fry small piece and taste; mixture should be highly seasoned. Adjust seasoning with salt and freshly ground pepper.

Preheat oven to 375°F. Line bottom and sides of 2-quart terrine mold with single layer of bacon. Spoon in meat mixture, packing firmly to eliminate air pockets. Cover with remaining bacon. Garnish with thyme and bay leaf. Cover and set in shallow roasting pan. Pour in enough water to come halfway up sides of mold. Bring to boil on top of stove. Bake until skewer inserted in center for 30 seconds is hot to touch, 1½ to 2 hours (water should be simmering throughout). Remove from water bath. Replace cover with waxed paper. Place 2-pound weight atop terrine and cool completely. Cover and refrigerate. (*Can be prepared 1 week ahead.*)

*Bones are optional; omit if unavailable.

2 ❧ Soups and Salads

Soups are an important part of the French diet. They are part of almost every meal, and the heartier ones often become the centerpiece dish at dinner. Sometimes they are quickly made of light stock and fresh vegetables; more often they are a nutritious, flavorful *potage* that is slow-simmered and served with plenty of bread or crisp buttered croutons.

With its simple peasant origins, French soup usually consists of inexpensive, flavorful vegetables such as leeks, garlic, onions, turnips, potatoes and carrots—all generously seasoned with herbs. Wild mushrooms or dried beans are sometimes added for more flavor and texture. For updated versions of country classics, try Normandy-style Apple and Root Vegetable Soup (page 18), Two-Bean Soup (page 19) or Green Herb Soup with Polenta Garnish (page 23) from the mountains of Savoy.

Another popular type of soup, one with distinctive regional variations, is based on fish. Originally made up of whatever was not sold from the day's catch, those humble broths have now become the rich, celebrated seafood soups such as Brittany Fish Soup (page 27), flavorful with vegetables, shrimp and chunks of salmon, and Niçoise Fish Soup (page 25) served with Rouille, a garlic mayonnaise spiked with hot red pepper, and toast slathered with Anchoiade, a tangy anchovy spread.

Salads are also an essential part of the meal, always served after the entrée as a palate refresher before dessert. Simple ones consist of garden-fresh greens dressed with a tangy vinaigrette or walnut oil. A good example of one of these would be Curly Endive Salad with Garlic Croutons (page 31) or Wilted Spinach and Lettuce Salad (page 31).

The French enjoy more elaborate "composed" salads as first courses. Preserved meat, bacon or fish, wild mushrooms or marinated vegetables may be the focus here, with leafy greens kept to minimum. Our versions include Wild Mushroom Salad (page 28), Scallop and Watercress Salad (page 29) and Two-Cabbage Salad with Tuna (page 30).

Substantial main-dish salads, such as Sweet and Sour Chicken Salad (page 32), Duck and Potato Salad (page 33) and Mediterranean Potato Salad with Mussels and Shrimp (page 35), are perfect for a light supper entrée or a more lavish dinner buffet.

 *Soups*

Garlic Soup

8 servings

5 large garlic heads (unpeeled)
4 cups rich chicken stock

1 chicken breast
2 eggs

Fresh lemon juice
Salt and freshly ground pepper
1/2 cup carrot julienne
1/2 cup leek julienne
Minced fresh parsley

Gently simmer garlic in stock in medium saucepan 30 minutes. Cool completely. Cover and chill overnight.

Remove garlic from stock and reserve for another use. Heat stock until gently shaking. Add chicken and poach just until firm and opaque, about 15 minutes. Skin, bone and shred chicken. Bring stock to simmer; degrease. Beat eggs to blend in small bowl. Whisk 1/4 cup stock into eggs. Whisk mixture back into saucepan. Remove from heat. Season with lemon juice, salt and pepper. Garnish with chicken, carrot, leek and parsley.

Apple and Root Vegetable Soup

4 main-course servings

10 cups water
1 pound leeks, white and pale green parts only, cut into 1 1/2-inch pieces
1 pound baking potatoes, peeled and cut into 1 1/2-inch pieces
3/4 pound carrots, peeled and cut into 1 1/2-inch pieces
1/2 pound sweet apples (such as Rome Beauty or Golden Delicious), peeled, cored and cut into 1 1/2-inch pieces

1 tablespoon salt
3 bay leaves
1 teaspoon coriander seeds
1/4 teaspoon whole black peppercorns

2 cups fresh parsley, minced
1/2 cup extra-virgin olive oil
1 large garlic clove, minced

Combine water, leeks, potatoes, carrots, apples, salt and bay leaves in large pot. Tie coriander seeds and peppercorns in cheesecloth and add to pot. Bring mixture to boil. Cover and simmer until vegetables are tender, stirring occasionally, about 45 minutes.

Using slotted spoon, transfer vegetables to processor and puree. Transfer puree to saucepan set over medium heat. Add enough of vegetable cooking liquid (about 2 1/2 cups) to make thick soup and heat through.

Mix parsley, oil and garlic. Ladle soup into bowls. Swirl some of parsley mixture into each bowl and serve.

Two-Bean Soup

Makes about 6 cups

½ pound (1½ cups) dried white beans, sorted

¼ pound salt pork

½ cup (1 stick) butter

2 medium leeks (white and light green parts), finely chopped

1 medium yellow onion, finely chopped

7 cups (about) cold light chicken stock

1 bouquet garni (12 parsley sprigs, 1 bay leaf and ½ teaspoon dried thyme, crumbled)

½ teaspoon dried savory, crumbled

Salt and freshly ground pepper

¼ pound small green beans, sliced diagonally 1/16 inch thick

¼ cup whipping cream

4 thin bacon slices, cooked crisp and crumbled

Cover dried white beans generously with water and soak overnight.

Cover salt pork with cold water and boil 2 minutes. Drain. Cut into ¼-inch cubes. Heat ¼ cup butter in heavy 4-quart saucepan over medium-low heat. Add salt pork and cook until golden, about 15 minutes. Transfer pork to plate, using slotted spoon. Add leeks and onion to pan and cook until translucent, about 10 minutes, stirring occasionally. Increase heat to medium-high and continue cooking uncovered until vegetables are golden, stirring frequently. Return pork to pan and let cool completely.

Rinse white beans and drain. Add to salt pork mixture. Blend in 6 cups stock and bring to boil slowly over medium heat. Add bouquet garni and savory. Reduce heat, cover partially and simmer soup until beans are tender and almost falling apart, about 1½ hours, adding more stock if necesary.

Discard bouquet garni. Puree soup in batches in blender. Strain through sieve into clean saucepan (soup should have consistency of heavy cream; add remaining stock if necessary). Season with salt and pepper. (*Can be prepared ahead to this point, cooled and refrigerated. Reheat before continuing.*)

Blanch green beans in boiling salted water 2 minutes. Whip cream until semistiff peaks form. Fold in bacon, then continue folding until cream stiffens. Season with salt and pepper. Mix remaining ¼ cup butter into hot soup. Ladle soup into bowls. Garnish with green beans and generous dollop of bacon-flavored whipped cream.

Cauliflower Soup with Cinnamon

4 servings

4 tablespoons butter

1 pound cauliflower, chopped

2 small boiling potatoes, peeled and coarsely chopped

½ teaspoon cinnamon

Salt and freshly ground pepper

4 cups water

¼ cup (or more) whipping cream

Snipped fresh chives

Melt 3 tablespoons butter in heavy medium saucepan over medium-high heat. Add cauliflower and potatoes and cook until just softened, stirring frequently, 10 to 12 minutes. Stir in ¼ teaspoon cinnamon. Season with salt and pepper. Add water, cover and bring to boil. Reduce heat and simmer until vegetables are tender, 15 minutes.

Transfer soup to blender and puree. Return to saucepan and bring to boil, stirring constantly. Reduce heat, add ¼ cup cream and simmer, stirring constantly, 2 to 3 minutes. (Add more cream if thinner consistency is desired.) Adjust seasoning. Garnish servings with remaining butter, cinnamon and chives.

Fennel Soup with Crème Fraîche and Bacon Lardons

This subtle soup makes an elegant opener for a dinner party.

6 servings

10 ounces slab bacon, rind trimmed, cut into ¼-inch cubes
Vegetable oil (optional)
2 cups chopped onions
4 cups coarsely chopped trimmed fennel (about 4 medium bulbs)
6 cups chicken stock

1 cup plus 9 tablespoons Crème Fraîche*
Salt and freshly ground pepper
⅓ cup snipped fresh chives or chopped green onion (green part only)

Cook bacon in heavy Dutch oven over medium heat until golden brown, stirring occasionally, about 10 minutes. Transfer to paper towels using slotted spoon. If necessary, add enough oil to pan drippings to measure ¼ cup. Heat over medium heat. Add onions and cook 4 minutes, stirring frequently. Add fennel and cook 5 minutes, stirring frequently. Add stock. Simmer until vegetables are tender, 35 to 40 minutes. Puree soup in batches in processor or blender until smooth. (*Can be prepared 1 day ahead and refrigerated.*)

Reheat soup over medium heat, stirring frequently. Whisk in 1 cup crème fraîche. Season with salt and pepper. Ladle soup into heated bowls. Spoon 1½ tablespoons crème fraîche atop each. Garnish with bacon and chives.

*Crème Fraîche

Makes about 2 cups

1½ cups whipping cream   ½ cup sour cream

Blend cream and sour cream in medium bowl. Cover and let stand at room temperature until thickened to consistency of sour cream, about 6 hours. Refrigerate until ready to use.

Wild Mushroom Soup

4 to 6 servings

½ cup brandy
1 ounce dried morels, rinsed
1 ounce dried cèpes, rinsed

5 tablespoons unsalted butter
1½ cups minced onions
½ pound button mushrooms, thinly sliced

½ pound fresh shiitake mushrooms, thinly sliced
2½ cups (or more) rich chicken or duck stock
½ cup (or more) whipping cream
Salt and freshly ground pepper
Fresh lemon juice

Heat brandy in heavy small saucepan. Add dried mushrooms and let stand until softened, about 30 minutes. Drain, reserving liquid. Rinse mushrooms; squeeze dry. Strain mushroom soaking liquid through sieve lined with several layers of dampened cheesecloth.

Melt butter in heavy medium saucepan over medium-low heat. Add onions and cook until translucent, stirring occasionally, about 10 minutes. Add fresh mushrooms and cook 15 minutes, stirring occasionally. Add dried mushrooms, soaking liquid and 2½ cups stock and simmer gently 45 minutes to thicken soup and blend flavors. Puree in blender. Return puree to saucepan. Add ½ cup cream. Season with salt, pepper and lemon juice. Thin with more stock or cream if desired. (*Can be prepared 2 days ahead and refrigerated. Reheat before serving.*)

Chanterelle Hazelnut Soup

6 servings

1 quart whipping cream
1¼ pounds fresh chanterelles or button mushrooms, chopped
1 cup hazelnuts, toasted, husked and coarsely chopped
5 large garlic cloves, flattened
2 medium shallots, quartered

2 cups unsalted chicken stock
½ cup dry Sherry
Salt and freshly ground pepper

1 tablespoon unsalted butter
¼ pound fresh chanterelles or button mushrooms, sliced
2 teaspoons dry vermouth
Snipped fresh chives

Combine cream, 1¼ pounds mushrooms, ¾ cup hazelnuts (reserve remainder for garnish), garlic and shallots in large nonaluminum saucepan. Cook over medium-high heat until reduced by half, stirring frequently, about 40 minutes. Cool.

Boil stock and Sherry in heavy large saucepan until reduced to 1 cup, about 10 minutes. Puree mushroom mixture through food mill fitted with medium disc. Stir into reduced stock. Season with salt and pepper. (*Can be prepared 1 day ahead and refrigerated.*)

Reheat soup over medium heat, stirring frequently. Melt butter in heavy small skillet over medium-high heat. Add ¼ pound mushrooms and cook until moisture evaporates, stirring frequently, about 5 minutes. Sprinkle with vermouth. Ladle soup into bowls. Garnish each serving with mushrooms, reserved hazelnuts and fresh chives.

Four-Onion Soup

8 servings

¼ cup (½ stick) butter
3 large onions, sliced
3 medium leeks (white and light green parts), sliced
1 bunch green onions, sliced (white part only)
¼ cup minced shallots
2 teaspoons minced fresh ginger
2 garlic cloves, crushed

Pinch of cayenne pepper
1 tablespoon all purpose flour
8 cups chicken stock
1 cup dry white wine
3 tablespoons brandy
1 teaspoon fresh lemon juice
1 teaspoon salt
Freshly ground pepper

Melt butter in heavy large saucepan over medium-high heat. Add onions, leeks, green onions, shallots, ginger and garlic and sauté until tender, about 20 minutes. Add cayenne and flour and stir until mixture is brown. Add stock and wine and simmer 20 minutes. Blend in brandy, juice, salt and pepper. Simmer 15 minutes. Serve Four-Onion Soup hot.

Crookneck Squash, Leek and Watercress Soup

This soup is smooth and gently spiced.

8 servings

¹/₄ cup (¹/₂ stick) unsalted butter
6 leeks (white part only), chopped
3 pounds yellow crookneck squash (trimmed), necks thinly sliced, remainder chopped
2 quarts (or more) chicken stock

Dash of hot pepper sauce
Salt and freshly ground pepper
2 bunches watercress, stemmed

Sour cream
Watercress leaves

Melt butter in heavy large saucepan over medium-low heat. Add leeks and cook until tender, stirring occasionally, about 10 minutes. Add chopped squash and stir 4 minutes. Add 2 quarts stock and simmer until squash is tender, about 15 minutes. Add hot pepper sauce. Season with salt and pepper. Add 2 bunches watercress and simmer 2 minutes. Puree soup in blender until smooth. (*Can be prepared 1 day ahead and refrigerated.*)

Just before serving, rewarm soup, thinning with more stock if desired. Ladle into heated bowls. Garnish with sliced squash, sour cream and watercress.

Cream of Butternut Squash and Leek Soup

6 to 8 servings

5 tablespoons unsalted butter
1³/₄ cups chopped leeks (white and light green parts)
4 pounds butternut squash, peeled, seeded and cut into 1-inch pieces
6 cups chicken stock
¹/₄ teaspoon dried thyme, crumbled
Salt

1 cup (or more) whipping cream
1 cup (or more) milk
Freshly ground white pepper
¹/₃ cup freshly grated Parmesan cheese
Chopped fresh chives or parsley

Melt butter in heavy large saucepan over medium-high heat. Add leeks and stir 4 minutes. Add squash and stir to coat with butter. Mix in stock, thyme and salt. Bring to boil. Reduce heat and simmer until squash is very tender, about 40 minutes.

Puree soup in batches in processor or blender. Return to saucepan. Mix in 1 cup cream and 1 cup milk. (*Can be prepared 1 day ahead and refrigerated.*) Rewarm soup over low heat, stirring constantly. Thin with more cream and milk if desired. Add pepper. Adjust seasoning. Ladle soup into bowls. Sprinkle with Parmesan. Garnish with chopped chives and serve.

Rich Vegetable and Bread Soup

4 servings

1 tablespoon unsalted butter
3 medium carrots, chopped
2 medium onions, chopped
6 cups rich duck or chicken stock

1 bay leaf
Salt and freshly ground pepper
8 day-old slices sourdough bread

Melt butter in heavy large saucepan over medium-low heat. Add carrots and onions and cook until just tender, stirring occasionally, about 15 minutes. Add stock, bay leaf and salt and pepper to taste and simmer until vegetables are tender, about 15 minutes. Place 2 slices of bread in each soup bowl. Ladle soup over and serve.

Creamy Tomato and Carrot Soup

Makes 2 quarts

¼ cup (½ stick) unsalted butter
1 tablespoon olive oil
1 medium onion, chopped
¾ pound carrots, chopped
1 medium tart green apple, peeled and chopped
2 teaspoons minced garlic
1 tablespoon light brown sugar
2½ pounds ripe tomatoes, peeled, seeded and coarsely chopped
4 cups (or more) chicken or vegetable stock, preferably homemade

1 tablespoon fresh lemon juice
1 teaspoon finely grated lemon peel
1 teaspoon curry powder
Bouquet garni (10 peppercorns, 4 cloves, 4 allspice berries, 2 bay leaves and 2 thyme sprigs)

1 cup whipping cream
Salt

Melt butter with olive oil in heavy large nonaluminum saucepan over medium heat. Add onion and cook until just translucent, stirring occasionally, about 10 minutes. Add carrots, apple and garlic and stir until softened and just beginning to color, about 10 minutes. Blend in brown sugar and cook 2 minutes. Add tomatoes, stock, lemon juice, peel, curry powder and bouquet garni. Reduce heat, cover partially and simmer until thickened, 45 minutes.

Discard bouquet garni. Puree soup in processor or food mill until almost smooth (a little texture should remain). Transfer to clean saucepan. Blend in whipping cream. Rewarm gently over low heat. Season with salt.

To serve chilled, puree soup, then refrigerate at least 2 hours. Thin with additional stock if desired. Whip cream to very soft peaks. Ladle soup into bowls. Top with gently whipped cream and serve.

Green Herb Soup with Polenta Garnish

Makes 3 quarts

Garnish
2 tablespoons (¼ stick) butter
1 cup water
2 cups cold milk
¾ cup yellow cornmeal
1 ¼-inch-thick prosciutto slice, cut into ¼-inch cubes
3 tablespoons minced fresh parsley
1 garlic clove, minced
Salt and freshly ground pepper

Green Herb Soup
¼ cup (½ stick) butter
4 large onions, finely chopped
3 large leeks, trimmed of dark green leaves, finely sliced
5 large garlic cloves, minced
2 quarts chicken stock, preferably homemade

2 small turnips, peeled, halved lengthwise and thinly sliced
1 carrot, peeled, halved lengthwise and thinly sliced
½ pound spinach leaves, stemmed, rolled up and cut into thin strips
1 medium cucumber, peeled, halved lengthwise, seeded and thinly sliced
1 medium zucchini, halved lengthwise and thinly sliced
½ cup minced fresh parsley
½ cup minced fresh chervil*
1 teaspoon dried marjoram, crumbled
Salt and freshly ground pepper

1 cup grated Emmenthal cheese

For garnish: Coat 8 × 8-inch metal pan with 1 tablespoon butter. Bring water to boil in heavy medium saucepan over medium heat. Mix milk with cornmeal in medium bowl. Stir into boiling water. Continue stirring until cornmeal is thick enough for spoon to stay upright, about 10 minutes. Blend in prosciutto, parsley, remaining 1 tablespoon butter, garlic, salt and pepper. Pour into prepared pan, smoothing to even thickness. Let cool to set completely. Cut into 1/2-inch cubes.

For soup: Melt 1/4 cup butter in stockpot over low heat. Add onions, leeks and garlic and cook until translucent, stirring occasionally, about 20 minutes. Add chicken stock, increase heat and bring to boil. Reduce heat to medium. Add turnips and carrot and cook until vegetables are very soft, about 30 minutes. Mix in spinach, cucumber, zucchini, parsley, chervil, marjoram and salt and pepper to taste and cook until tender, 5 to 10 minutes.

Add polenta cubes to soup. Ladle into bowls. Pass cheese separately.

*If unavailable, 2 to 4 tablespoons minced fresh tarragon or mint can be substituted.

Oyster Cream Soup

The shucked oysters will yield enough "liquor" to strain and use in this soup.

8 servings

3 tablespoons unsalted butter
2 medium onions, chopped
1 bunch green onions (white part only), chopped
3 large garlic cloves, minced
2 medium tomatoes, peeled, seeded and chopped
1 teaspoon minced fresh basil leaves
1 teaspoon minced fresh thyme leaves

Salt and freshly ground white pepper
Cayenne pepper

4 cups whipping cream, boiled until reduced to 3 cups
1/2 cup strained oyster liquor
2 cups half and half
3 cups shucked oysters (about 24)
Basil leaves

Melt butter in heavy medium saucepan over medium-low heat. Add onions and garlic and cook until transparent, stirring occasionally, about 10 minutes. Add tomatoes. Increase heat to medium and cook until thickened, stirring occasionally, about 10 minutes. Stir in basil and thyme. Season with salt, pepper and cayenne. Cook until all moisture has evaporated. Allow to cool completely. Cover. Chill overnight.

Puree onion mixture in processor. Transfer to heavy large saucepan. Add reduced cream and oyster liquor and bring to boil. Reduce heat. Add half and half and heat through. Adjust seasoning. Add oysters and poach until just opaque, about 2 minutes. Ladle into bowls. Garnish with basil leaves.

Mussel Soup with Corn

If mussels are not available, you can substitute clams.

6 servings

2 pounds mussels, scrubbed and debearded
1/2 cup dry white wine
2 shallots, minced

2 tablespoons (1/4 stick) unsalted butter
1 large leek, white and light green parts only, minced
1 medium onion, minced

2 1/4 cups (about) milk

6 egg yolks, room temperature
1/2 cup whipping cream

1 1/3 cups fresh corn kernels (about 2 ears), cooked until tender
1/2 cup watercress leaves, blanched 1 minute
Salt

Combine mussels, wine and shallots in heavy large saucepan over high heat. Cover and cook until mussels open, shaking pan occasionally, about 4 minutes. Remove opened mussels. Cook unopened mussels 3 more minutes. Discard remaining unopened mussels. Let cooking liquid stand 15 minutes to allow sand to fall to bottom.

Shell mussels, discarding shells. Pull off rubbery ring around each mussel. Strain liquid through sieve lined with 2 layers of dampened cheesecloth.

Melt butter in heavy large saucepan over medium-low heat. Add leek and onion and cook until very tender, stirring occasionally, about 15 minutes.

Measure mussel liquid. Add enough milk to total 3 cups. Add to leek mixture and cook over medium heat until warmed through; do not boil.

Whisk yolks and cream in small bowl. Whisk in about ½ cup milk mixture. Return to leek mixture and stir over low heat until thick enough to leave path when finger is drawn across back of spoon; do not boil.

Add mussels, corn and watercress. Season with salt. Serve hot or cold.

Niçoise Fish Soup with Anchoiade and Rouille

6 main-course servings

2 medium garlic cloves, peeled

2 small carrots, peeled, scored and cut into feed-tube lengths
1 small onion, peeled

2 small celery stalks (strings removed), cut into feed-tube lengths
1 fennel stalk (strings removed), cut into feed-tube lengths

4 cups Fish Stock*
¾ teaspoon salt
    Freshly ground pepper
36 haricots verts or baby green beans, trimmed, halved and steamed until crisp-tender

18 Niçoise olives
1 tomato, peeled, seeded and diced
1 tablespoon Cognac
⅛ teaspoon saffron threads

    Anchoiade**
6 slices toasted French bread
3 cups Fish Stock*
5 whole flounder (4½ to 5 pounds total), skinned and boned (bones reserved for Fish Stock), cut into 2 × 3-inch pieces
    Rouille***

Insert steel knife in processor. With machine running, drop garlic through feed tube and mince. Leave in work bowl.

Insert thin slicer. Stand carrots in feed tube and slice using firm pressure. Stand onion in feed tube and slice using firm pressure. Leave in work bowl.

Insert medium slicer. Stand celery and fennel stalks in feed tube and then slice vegetables using medium pressure.

Transfer contents of work bowl to heavy 2½-quart saucepan. Add 4 cups Fish Stock, salt and pepper. Bring to boil. Reduce heat and simmer until vegetables are crisp-tender, about 8 minutes. Add green beans, olives, tomato, Cognac and saffron; keep warm.

Meanwhile, spread Anchoiade on toast. Bring 3 cups Fish Stock to gentle simmer in heavy 8-inch skillet. Add fish in batches and cook until just opaque, 1½ to 2 minutes. Transfer fish to heated soup bowls, using slotted spatula. Ladle vegetables and broth over. Garnish with toasted French bread. Pass Rouille separately.

*Fish Stock

Makes about 7¹/₂ cups

1 medium onion, peeled and quartered

1 small leek, white part only, cut into feed-tube lengths

1 large celery stalk, cut into feed-tube lengths

Fish bones reserved from soup
8 whole peppercorns

3 parsley stems
1 bay leaf
1 fresh thyme sprig or ¹/₈ teaspoon dried thyme, crumbled
7¹/₂ cups water
1 cup dry white wine

Coarsely chop onion in processor using about 3 on/off turns. Remove steel knife and insert medium slicer.

Stand leek and celery in feed tube and slice using medium pressure.

Transfer onion-leek mixture to heavy 8-quart pot. Add fish bones, peppercorns, parsley, bay leaf and thyme. Cover with waxed paper round and cook over low heat until moisture appears, about 5 minutes. Discard paper. Add water and wine and bring to boil, skimming surface occasionally. Reduce heat and simmer 30 minutes. Strain liquid into large bowl. Let stand at room temperature 1 hour or refrigerate overnight; do not stir. Ladle out clear stock; discard any residue.

**Anchoiade

A smooth, anchovy-based spread.

Makes about ¹/₃ cup

1 large garlic clove, peeled
1 2-ounce can flat anchovies, rinsed and patted dry

1 egg yolk
Freshly ground pepper
3 tablespoons olive oil

With machine running, drop garlic through processor feed tube and mince. Add anchovies, yolk and pepper and blend until smooth. With machine running, slowly drizzle oil through feed tube in slow, steady stream and process until thick, about 5 seconds. (*Can be made 2 days ahead, covered and refrigerated.*)

***Rouille

Harissa powder is available in ethnic and specialty foods stores. If unavailable, combine 1¹/₂ teaspoons cayenne pepper, ³/₄ teaspoon ground cumin and ¹/₈ teaspoon salt. Use 1 teaspoon in recipe; store remainder in jar.

Makes about 1²/₃ cups

5 medium garlic cloves, peeled
3 ounces red-skinned potatoes, boiled until tender, peeled
1 egg
1 teaspoon harissa powder

1 teaspoon Hungarian sweet paprika
³/₄ teaspoon salt
¹/₈ teaspoon cayenne pepper
1 cup olive oil

Insert steel knife in processor. With machine running, drop garlic through feed tube and mince. Add potatoes, egg, harissa powder, paprika, salt, pepper and 3 tablespoons oil and process until slightly thickened, about 10 seconds. With machine running, slowly drizzle remaining oil through feed tube in slow, steady stream (once mixture has thickened, oil can be added more quickly). Adjust seasoning. (*Can be prepared 3 days ahead, covered and refrigerated.*)

Brittany Fish Soup

8 to 10 servings

Soup Base
4 pounds fish bones, cleaned and rinsed
1½ quarts water
2 cups clam juice
1¼ cups Muscadet
4 large onions, sliced
1 small carrot, sliced
Bouquet garni (12 parsley sprigs, 1 bay leaf and ½ teaspoon dried thyme, crumbled)

1½ pounds salmon steaks, boned (bones reserved) and skinned
1 pound halibut steaks, boned (bones reserved) and skinned
1 pound thick sole or flounder fillets
1 pound sea scallops

12 large shrimp, peeled (shells reserved) and deveined
1 tablespoon *each* minced fresh chervil, chives, parsley and tarragon, or 1 teaspoon *each* dried, crumbled
2 tablespoons fresh lemon juice

¼ pound cauliflower
¼ pound broccoli

1 pound mussels, scrubbed and debearded
2 medium shallots, minced

¾ cup whipping cream
¼ cup sour cream
Salt and freshly ground pepper

For soup base: Break fish bones into small pieces. Place in stockpot with 1½ quarts water, clam juice, 1 cup Muscadet, onions, carrot and bouquet garni. Bring to boil, then reduce heat and simmer 35 to 40 minutes, mashing bones with wooden spoon to release flavor. Ladle mixture through strainer lined with several layers of dampened cheesecloth. Return liquid to pot.

Cut salmon and halibut into ½-inch cubes. Cut sole into ½-inch-wide strips. Quarter scallops. Combine fish, scallops and shrimp in large glass dish. Sprinkle with herbs and lemon juice. Marinate in refrigerator while preparing soup. Add reserved shrimp shells and fish bones to strained soup base.

Cut cauliflower and broccoli florets into ½-inch pieces. Peel stems and cut into 1-inch chunks. Blanch cauliflower in boiling salted water until crisp-tender. Remove with slotted spoon. Repeat with broccoli. Add 1 cup vegetable cooking liquid to soup base.

Combine mussels, remaining ¼ cup Muscadet and shallots in small saucepan. Cover and steam 5 minutes over medium-high heat. Remove opened mussels to bowl using slotted spoon. Continue cooking remaining mussels about 5 minutes. Discard any that do not open. Reserve steaming liquid. Remove mussels from shells, discarding shells. Ladle reserved liquid through strainer lined with several layers of dampened cheesecloth into soup base.

Bring soup base to boil. Reduce heat and simmer until reduced to about 5¼ cups. Ladle through strainer lined with several layers of dampened cheesecloth into clean saucepan.

Place marinated fish, scallops and shrimp in large Dutch oven. Bring soup base to boil and pour over fish mixture. Turn heat to medium-high. Add mussels, vegetables and whipping cream and heat through; *do not boil*. Blend ½ cup soup into sour cream, then return to soup. Season with salt and pepper.

🍎 Salads

Wild Mushroom Salad

Use only the tender inner leaves of curly endive for this appetizer.

6 to 8 servings

1½ bunches mâche (lamb's lettuce)
1 head limestone or butter lettuce
1 head curly endive
1 small head radicchio
1 bunch arugula, leaves only
½ bunch watercress, leaves only

¼ pound fresh chanterelle mushrooms
¼ pound fresh oyster mushrooms
¼ pound fresh shiitake mushrooms

4 tablespoons walnut oil
2 tablespoons pine nuts
1 large shallot, minced
3 medium garlic cloves, minced
2 tablespoons Sherry wine vinegar
1 tablespoon minced fresh basil
1 tablespoon minced fresh tarragon
1 tablespoon minced fresh thyme
1 tablespoon snipped fresh chives
Salt and freshly ground pepper

Tear mâche, limestone lettuce, curly endive and radicchio into bite-size pieces. Transfer to bowl. Mix in arugula and watercress leaves.

Slice mushrooms into bite-size pieces if necessary. Heat 2 tablespoons oil in heavy large skillet over high heat. Add mushrooms and cook until just tender but firm to bite, about 2 minutes; do not allow mushrooms to release liquid. Set aside ⅓ of mushrooms for garnish. Sprinkle remainder over greens. Heat remaining 2 tablespoons oil in same skillet over high heat. Add pine nuts and stir until golden brown. Add shallot and garlic and stir 1 minute. Stir in vinegar. Add herbs. Season with salt and pepper. Pour over salad. Divide among plates. Top each with some of reserved mushrooms and serve.

Beet Salad with Marinated Turnip Slices

4 to 6 servings

18 ounces turnips (about 4 small), peeled, trimmed and sliced about ⅛ inch thick

2 tablespoons white wine vinegar
⅛ teaspoon cumin seeds
Salt and freshly ground pepper
9 tablespoons olive oil

3 tablespoons red wine vinegar
½ teaspoon minced garlic
1½ pounds beets (about 5 small), peeled and finely grated
2 large shallots, thinly sliced

1 hard-cooked egg yolk
2 teaspoons minced fresh tarragon

Blanch turnips in boiling salted water 1 minute. Drain; pat dry.

Blend white wine vinegar, cumin seeds and salt and pepper in large bowl. Whisk in 5 tablespoons oil in thin stream. Add turnips and toss well. Cover and refrigerate 15 minutes.

Blend red wine vinegar, garlic and salt and pepper in large bowl. Whisk in remaining 4 tablespoons oil. Add beets and shallots and toss well.

Mound beet salad in center of platter. Surround with overlapping turnip slices. Sieve yolk over beets. Garnish with tarragon. Serve immediately.

Warm Mussel Salad with Shallot Dressing

6 servings

6 cups mixed salad greens, such as
 Romaine and red leaf lettuce,
 watercress, mâche, arugula and
 radish greens, torn into bite-size
 pieces

2 cups dry white wine
2 medium onions, quartered
1 celery stalk, chopped
4 parsley sprigs
1 bay leaf
¹/₂ teaspoon dried thyme, crumbled
3 pounds mussels, scrubbed and
 debearded

Dressing
1 cup olive oil
¹/₃ cup chopped fresh parsley
2 tablespoons fresh lemon juice
2 tablespoons minced shallots
1 garlic clove, minced
 Dash of hot pepper sauce
 Salt and freshly ground pepper

Arrange mixed salad greens on serving plates. Set aside.

Combine wine, onions, celery, parsley sprigs, bay leaf and thyme in heavy large saucepan. Add mussels. Cover and cook over medium-high heat 5 minutes. Remove opened mussels. Cook remaining mussels about 5 more minutes; discard any that do not open. Discard top shells, leaving mussels in bottom shells. Arrange on greens.

For dressing: Combine all ingredients in heavy small saucepan. Whisk over low heat until warm. Spoon dressing over salads and serve.

Scallop and Watercress Salad

6 servings

4 small carrots, peeled and cut
 into julienne
3 small turnips, peeled and cut
 into julienne

36 sea scallops
6 tablespoons olive oil
2 tablespoons minced fresh parsley
 Salt and freshly ground pepper

 Olive oil
2 bunches (about) watercress,
 leaves only
 Chervil leaves
6 thin slices country-style
 bread, toasted

Blanch carrots and turnips separately in boiling salted water until crisp-tender; drain thoroughly.

Finely mince 10 scallops. Finely mince ¹/₄ cup *each* blanched carrot and turnip julienne. Mix minced scallops and minced vegetables in large bowl. Stir in 6 tablespoons olive oil and parsley. Season with salt and pepper.

Cut remaining scallops into paper-thin slices. Toss remaining carrot and turnip julienne with olive oil to coat. Season with salt and pepper. Mound vegetable julienne mixture in center of each plate. Top with minced scallop mixture. Alternate scallop slices and watercress leaves around vegetable mixture. Season with salt and pepper. Drizzle with olive oil. Garnish with chervil. Serve salads with thin toast.

Two-Cabbage Salad with Tuna

6 servings

7 tablespoons walnut oil
6 ounces fresh tuna, skinned and cut into 1 × ¹/₂ × ¹/₄-inch pieces
2 shallots, minced
¹/₂ small green cabbage, halved, cored and thinly sliced (about 5¹/₂ cups)

¹/₂ small red cabbage, halved, cored and thinly sliced (about 5¹/₂ cups)
¹/₃ cup red wine vinegar
Salt and freshly ground pepper
¹/₄ cup walnuts, finely chopped

Heat 3 tablespoons oil in heavy large skillet over high heat. Add tuna and sauté until golden, about 1 minute per side. Remove from skillet. Heat 2 more tablespoons oil in skillet. Add ¹/₃ of shallots and stir 1 minute. Add green cabbage and toss to coat with oil. Add half of vinegar, salt and pepper and cook until cabbage is slightly wilted, stirring occasionally, 2 to 3 minutes. Remove from skillet and arrange around edge of platter. Heat remaining oil in skillet. Add ¹/₃ of shallots and stir 1 minute. Add red cabbage and toss to coat with oil. Add remaining vinegar, salt and pepper and cook until cabbage is slightly wilted, 3 to 5 minutes. Remove from skillet and arrange in center of platter. Sprinkle cabbage with remaining shallots. Top red cabbage with tuna. Sprinkle walnuts over green cabbage and serve.

Escarole Salad with Bacon, Vegetables and Fried Onions

6 to 8 servings

5 ounces slab bacon, cut into 1 × 3-inch cubes

3 large red potatoes, cooked, peeled and thinly sliced
3 small turnips, peeled and cut into paper-thin slices
6 small onions, thinly sliced
Salt

3 tablespoons red wine vinegar
1¹/₂ teaspoons Dijon mustard

³/₄ cup vegetable oil
Freshly ground pepper
1 slice bread, toasted
1 garlic clove
2 small heads escarole, torn into bite-size pieces, wrapped in towel and refrigerated
¹/₂ cup cooked green peas
1¹/₂ teaspoons minced shallot
Minced fresh parsley

Cook bacon in heavy large skillet over medium-low heat until golden brown, but not crisp. Remove with slotted spoon and drain on paper towels.

Reheat bacon fat over medium-high heat. Add potatoes and fry on both sides until golden brown, about 5 minutes; do not overcook. Transfer to plate. Add turnips to skillet and cook on both sides until tender and golden brown, about 10 minutes. Add to potatoes. Reduce heat to medium. Add onions to skillet and cook until tender and golden brown, stirring occasionally, about 15 minutes. Add to other vegetables. Sprinkle with salt.

Stir vinegar into skillet, scraping up browned bits. Blend in mustard. Whisk in oil in thin stream. Season with salt and pepper. Strain dressing into large salad bowl. Rub toast with garlic. Rewhisk dressing. Add bacon, potatoes, turnips, onions, toast, escarole, peas and shallot to dressing and toss gently. Discard toast. Sprinkle salad with parsley and serve.

Wilted Spinach and Lettuce Salad

4 servings

Walnut Oil Dressing
  5 **ounces slab bacon, cut into**
     $^1/_3$ × 1-inch cubes
  3 **tablespoons white wine vinegar**
$1^1/_2$ **teaspoons Dijon mustard**
  9 **tablespoons walnut oil**
    Salt and freshly ground pepper

1 **head red leaf lettuce**
1 **pound spinach leaves, stemmed**
$^1/_3$ **cup chopped walnuts**
1 **large shallot, minced**

For dressing: Fry bacon in heavy medium skillet over low heat until golden but not crisp, stirring frequently. Drain on paper towels. Remove skillet from heat; discard bacon fat. Stir in vinegar to deglaze pan. Blend in mustard. Whisk in oil in slow steady stream until well emulsified. Season to taste with salt and pepper.

    Toss red lettuce with half of dressing in large bowl. Arrange on platter. Reheat remaining dressing in same skillet over medium-high heat. Add spinach and stir quickly to wilt; spinach should stay bright green. Spread spinach over red lettuce. Sprinkle with bacon, walnuts and shallot. Serve immediately.

Curly Endive Salad with Garlic Croutons

For a variation, top each serving of salad with a warm poached egg.

4 servings

1 **large head curly endive**
$^1/_2$ **pound salt pork, parboiled**
    5 minutes and rind removed

Croutons
12 **$^1/_4$- to $^1/_2$-inch-thick slices**
    French bread
    Olive oil
  2 **garlic cloves, halved**

Vinaigrette
$^1/_4$ **cup red wine vinegar**
  2 **medium shallots, minced**
  1 **tablespoon Dijon mustard**
    Salt and freshly ground pepper
$^1/_2$ **cup olive oil**

Tear endive coarsely into salad bowl. Cover with damp towel and refrigerate. Slice salt pork $^1/_3$ inch thick. Cut crosswise into strips $^1/_3$ inch wide. Sauté in heavy small skillet over medium heat until brown and crisp. Transfer to paper towels. Pour off all but $^1/_4$ cup drippings in skillet.

    For croutons: Position rack in center of oven and preheat to 400°F. Arrange bread slices in single layer on baking sheet. Brush tops with oil. Bake until just golden, 5 to 10 minutes, watching carefully. Rub both sides of bread with cut edge of garlic. Quarter slices.

    For vinaigrette: Mix vinegar, shallots, mustard, salt and pepper in small bowl. Whisk in oil 1 drop at a time.

    Before serving, heat reserved salt pork drippings. Toss endive with salt pork, croutons and vinaigrette. Mix in warmed drippings. Adjust seasoning.

Mixed Green Salad with Goat Cheese and Mustard Vinaigrette

8 servings

1/4 cup raspberry vinegar
4 teaspoons Dijon mustard
1 cup vegetable oil
1/4 teaspoon salt
  Freshly ground pepper

1 pound mixed greens
8 1/2-inch-thick slices goat cheese (preferably Montrachet)

Blend vinegar and mustard in processor. With machine running, slowly add oil through feed tube. Season with salt and freshly ground pepper.

Combine greens in large bowl. Add vinaigrette and toss. Arrange on plates. Top with 1 slice goat cheese.

Salad of Vodka-marinated Tomato and Green Beans

4 servings

1 pound green beans, trimmed and cut in 1 1/2-inch pieces

1 1/2 pounds ripe tomatoes, peeled, seeded and cut in eighths
1/4 cup vodka
  Salt and freshly ground pepper

3 tablespoons olive oil
1 teaspoon red wine vinegar
1/4 cup snipped fresh chives
1/3 cup minced fresh parsley
1 shallot, thinly sliced

Blanch green beans in boiling salted water 3 minutes. Rinse immediately under cold water. Drain; pat dry.

Combine green beans and tomatoes in large bowl. Toss with vodka and salt and freshly ground pepper. Let stand 2 hours, tossing occasionally.

Drain green beans and tomatoes. Return to bowl. Toss with oil and vinegar. Set aside 1 tablespoon chives. Add remaining chives, parsley and shallot to bowl and toss gently. Season with salt and pepper. Sprinkle with reserved chives.

Sweet and Sour Chicken Salad

Refreshing and tangy, this light main dish is pretty enough for company.

4 main-course servings

1 cup red grapes, halved, seeded and peeled (if desired)
1 cup chicken stock, preferably homemade
1 cup Chardonnay or dry white wine
1 tablespoon (or more) fresh lemon juice
  Salt and freshly ground pepper
1 tablespoon moutarde de Meaux or other coarse-grained French mustard

1 shallot, finely chopped and squeezed dry
5 tablespoons corn oil
1/4 cup hazelnut oil

4 skinned and boned chicken breast halves

1/2 pound spinach leaves, preferably small
2 curly endives, white center leaves only

Combine half of grapes, 1 cup stock, 3/4 cup wine, 1 tablespoon lemon juice, salt and pepper in blender and puree. Strain into heavy medium saucepan. Boil until reduced to 1/2 cup. Remove from heat. Blend in remaining wine, mustard, shallot, salt and pepper. Gradually whisk in oils in thin stream. Return dressing to blender.

Heat nonstick skillet over medium-high heat. Brush skillet with 1 tablespoon dressing. Add chicken and sear on one side. Turn, season with salt and pepper and sear on second side. Reduce heat to lowest setting and cook chicken until opaque and just firm to touch, about 5 minutes. Remove chicken from skillet. Cut diagonally into ½-inch strips. Transfer to bowl. Blend dressing until smooth. Add to chicken. Marinate 1 hour.

Add remaining grapes, spinach and endive leaves to chicken and toss well. Adjust seasoning with salt, pepper and lemon juice. Serve immediately.

Duck and Potato Salad

8 servings

24 unpeeled garlic cloves

12 1½- to 2-inch red boiling potatoes

¼ cup olive oil (preferably extra-virgin)

1 teaspoon coarsely ground pepper

½ teaspoon salt

1 4½-pound duck

1 orange, halved

½ pound fresh French or Polish garlic sausage

2 quarts water

Vinaigrette

⅓ cup red wine vinegar

5 teaspoons Dijon mustard

¾ cup olive oil (preferably extra-virgin)

¾ cup chopped Italian parsley

½ cup finely chopped red onion

½ cup black Niçoise olives

1 teaspoon coarsely ground pepper

1 savoy cabbage

Simmer garlic in water to cover 5 minutes. Drain and cool. Peel garlic.

Preheat oven to 400°F. Pierce potatoes all over with fork. Place in shallow baking pan. Coat with oil, 1 teaspoon pepper and ½ teaspoon salt. Pat duck dry. Pierce skin with fork. Rub inside and out with orange. Sprinkle generously with salt and pepper. Arrange breast side up in another roasting pan. Cook potatoes and duck 45 minutes, turning potatoes occasionally. Turn duck breast side down. Add garlic to duck. Continue cooking until duck is golden brown and juices run clear when pierced in thigh and potatoes are tender, turning potatoes and garlic occasionally, about 10 minutes longer. Transfer duck and garlic to platter and cool. Let potatoes cool.

Meanwhile, simmer sausage gently in 2 quarts water in medium saucepan until cooked through, about 40 minutes. Drain and cool. Skin sausage and cut into ½-inch-thick rounds. Halve each sausage round crosswise.

For vinaigrette: Mix vinegar and mustard in small bowl. Slowly whisk in oil.

Cut potatoes into ½-inch-thick slices. Combine with sausage, parsley, onion, olives and 1 teaspoon pepper in large bowl. Mix in vinaigrette.

Skin and bone duck. Cut meat into 2½-inch shreds. Add duck and garlic to salad. Season with salt and pepper. Let stand at room temperature 1 hour.

Line large platter with cabbage leaves. Spoon salad over and serve.

Warm White Bean and Lamb Sausage Salad

Serve barely warm, topped with the crisp lamb sausages. Accompany with a loaf of country bread and a bottle of spicy red Zinfandel or Beaujolais.

6 main-course servings

White Bean Salad
1 1/2 cups dried Great Northern beans, rinsed and sorted

1/3 cup olive oil
1 cup coarsely chopped celery
1 large green bell pepper, cored, seeded and coarsely chopped
1 large onion, coarsely chopped
1 1/2 teaspoons ground cumin
1/2 teaspoon freshly ground pepper
1/2 teaspoon cinnamon
1/4 teaspoon ground allspice
1/3 cup dried currants, rinsed in warm water and drained
1/4 cup tomato paste
1/4 cup Sherry wine vinegar

1 cup packed fresh Italian parsley leaves and tender stems
3 medium garlic cloves

2 teaspoons salt
1/2 cup olive oil

Bitter Green Salad
2 tablespoons Sherry wine vinegar
1 tablespoon dry Sherry
3/4 teaspoon salt
    Pinch of sugar
    Freshly ground pepper
5 tablespoons olive oil
6 cups assorted greens, such as escarole, curly endive, arugula and dandelion

1 tablespoon olive oil
    Lamb Sausages*

    Cherry tomatoes
    Lemon wedges

For bean salad: Place beans in large bowl. Add cold water to cover by 3 inches and let soak overnight.

Drain beans. Place in heavy large saucepan. Add cold water to cover. Cover and simmer until beans are tender, stirring occasionally, about 75 minutes. Drain. (*Can be prepared 1 day ahead, covered and refrigerated.*)

Heat 1/3 cup oil in heavy large skillet over medium-high heat. Add celery, green pepper and onion and cook until vegetables are golden brown, stirring frequently, about 10 minutes. Reduce heat to medium. Add cumin, pepper, cinnamon and allspice and stir 1 1/2 minutes. Mix in currants, tomato paste and vinegar and cook 5 minutes, stirring frequently. Reduce heat to low. Add beans and cook 20 minutes to blend flavors, stirring occasionally. Transfer mixture to large bowl.

Place parsley, garlic and salt in processor and chop finely using on/off turns. With machine running, gradually add 1/2 cup oil in thin steady stream. Stir parsley mixture into warm beans. Let stand 30 to 45 minutes.

For bitter green salad: Combine vinegar, Sherry, salt, sugar and pepper in small bowl. Gradually whisk in 5 tablespoons oil in thin steady stream. Mix greens in another bowl.

Heat 1 tablespoon oil in heavy large skillet over medium-high heat. Add sausages and cook until brown on all sides and barely pink inside, shaking pan occasionally, about 8 minutes. Transfer to plate. Let stand 5 minutes.

Toss greens with dressing to taste. Line large shallow bowl with greens. Mound beans in center. Top with sausages. Garnish with tomatoes and lemon wedges. Serve immediately.

*Lamb Sausages

Makes about 18

1½ pounds ground lamb
¾ cup finely minced onion
⅔ cup minced fresh parsley
½ cup minced fresh cilantro
½ cup minced green onions (white and green parts)
⅓ cup fine dry white breadcrumbs
1 egg, beaten to blend
3 tablespoons minced fresh mint

2 tablespoons fresh lemon juice
1 tablespoon plus 2 teaspoons Hungarian sweet paprika
1 tablespoon grated lemon peel
2 large garlic cloves, minced
1½ teaspoons salt
1 teaspoon ground cumin
¼ teaspoon cayenne pepper
Freshly ground pepper

Combine all ingredients in large bowl. Mix well. Cover bowl and refrigerate for 12 hours or overnight.

Line baking sheet with waxed paper. Using wet hands, shape ¼ cup mixture between palms into 2½-inch-long 1¼-inch-wide sausage. Repeat with remaining sausage mixture. Set on prepared baking sheet. Cover and chill 1 hour. (*Can be prepared 8 hours ahead.*)

Mediterranean Potato Salad with Mussels and Shrimp

Colorful potatoes, peppers, shrimp and mussels on a bed of arugula and endive. Partner with a hearty red wine and crusty garlic bread.

6 main-course servings

3 large red bell peppers
2 large yellow bell peppers

2½ to 3 pounds very small red potatoes, skinned
6 tablespoons dry white wine
1 cup thinly sliced red onion
⅓ cup minced fresh parsley
Sun-dried Tomato Dressing*

¾ cup dry white wine
24 mussels, scrubbed and debearded

2 tablespoons olive oil
18 uncooked large shrimp, peeled and deveined (tails left intact)
2 small garlic cloves, minced
Pinch of Hungarian sweet paprika
Salt and freshly ground black pepper

1 large bunch arugula
1 small head curly endive, torn into large pieces
18 Kalamata olives

Char peppers over gas flame or in broiler until blackened on all sides. Wrap in paper bag and let stand 10 minutes to steam. Peel and seed. Rinse if necessary; pat dry. Reserve half of red bell pepper for dressing. Cut remaining peppers lengthwise into eighths. (*Can be prepared 4 hours ahead.*)

Cook potatoes in large pot of boiling salted water until knife inserted into center of potato goes through easily, about 30 minutes. Drain potatoes. Transfer to large bowl. Pour 6 tablespoons wine over. Add onion, parsley and ⅔ of dressing and toss well. Cover and let stand for 2 hours.

Combine ¾ cup wine and mussels in heavy large pot over medium-high heat. Cover and steam 5 minutes. Remove opened mussels. Cook remaining mussels about 5 more minutes; discard any that do not open. Discard empty shell halves. Transfer mussels to bowl. Cool to lukewarm.

Heat 2 tablespoons oil in heavy large skillet over medium-high heat. Pat shrimp dry. Add to skillet. Sprinkle with garlic, paprika, salt and pepper and cook until shrimp are just pink, turning occasionally, 2 to 3 minutes. Transfer to bowl. Cool slightly.

Line large platter with arugula and curly endive. Mound potatoes in center.

Arrange red and yellow pepper slices around potatoes. Garnish platter with mussels on the half shell, shrimp and olives. Drizzle additional dressing over mussels and shrimp.

*Sun-dried Tomato Dressing

Makes about 1³/₄ cups

4 ounces sun-dried tomatoes in oil, drained and finely chopped
¹/₂ roasted red bell pepper, chopped (reserved from Mediterranean Potato Salad)
¹/₃ cup pitted Kalamata olives

2 garlic cloves, minced
¹/₂ teaspoon salt
¹/₃ cup red wine vinegar
2 tablespoons balsamic vinegar
³/₄ cup olive oil

Blend tomatoes, bell pepper, olives, garlic and salt to coarse puree in processor, stopping occasionally to scrape down sides of work bowl. With machine running, gradually add both vinegars. Add oil in thin steady stream until blended. (*Dressing can be prepared 1 day ahead and refrigerated. Bring to room temperature before using.*)

3 ❦ Eggs and Cheese

With typical resourcefulness, the French make the most out of very basic ingredients. A simple egg becomes an elegant first course or luncheon or supper entrée (eggs are seldom prepared for breakfast). And milk, in plentiful supply in regions throughout the country, is made into cheeses of every kind (see A Glossary of French Cheeses, page 40), from Camembert and Neufchâtel in Normandy and Munster and Gruyère from the eastern mountain regions, to the world-class Roquefort of the Languedoc and Brie from the Ile de France.

The French enjoy eggs in an endless number of ways. We offer a few of them, from the easiest, such as Bacon-Onion Baked Eggs (page 38), to the sublime, in our rich, Burgundy-style omelet (page 39) brimming with bacon, snails, mushrooms and wine.

Although served as a separate course at formal occasions, cheese is also frequently enjoyed as a snack with bread, or as a dessert with fruit and wine. Cooked with other ingredients, it adds creaminess, flavor and substance to many other dishes, such as the Leek and Swiss Chard Gratin (page 40), Eggplant and Parmesan Soufflé (page 42) and Spinach Chèvre Walnut Tart (page 44).

Bacon-Onion Baked Eggs

2 to 4 servings

2 tablespoons (¼ stick) butter
1 pound onions, halved and
  thinly sliced
¾ teaspoon minced fresh thyme, or
  ¼ teaspoon dried, crumbled
  Salt and freshly ground pepper

1 teaspoon white wine vinegar
4 eggs
4 tablespoons (½ stick) butter,
  melted
3 slices bacon, cut crosswise into
  ¼-inch strips

Melt 2 tablespoons butter in heavy large skillet over medium-low heat. Stir in onions, thyme, salt and pepper. Cover and cook until tender, stirring frequently, about 20 minutes. Uncover, increase heat to medium and cook until light brown, stirring frequently, about 5 minutes. (*Can be prepared 1 day ahead. Cover and refrigerate.*)

Position rack in center of oven and preheat to 400°F. Butter four 6-inch shallow baking dishes or one 8x1-inch round dish. Heat in oven until dishes are hot, about 2 minutes.

Meanwhile, reheat onion mixture over medium-low heat until very hot, stirring frequently. Stir in vinegar. Taste and adjust seasoning. Divide among small dishes or spread in bottom of large dish. Make well in center of each dish using small spoon, or make 4 wells in large dish. Break 1 egg into small bowl and then slide into well, being careful not to break yolk; repeat, adding 1 egg to each well. Spoon 1 tablespoon melted butter over each egg. For very soft eggs, bake 5 minutes for small dishes or 8 minutes for large dish. Check and continue cooking until eggs are set as desired.

Meanwhile, cook bacon in heavy small skillet over medium-low heat until light brown and crisp, about 6 minutes. Drain on paper towels. Sprinkle bacon around cooked eggs. Set dishes on plates and serve immediately.

Baked Eggs with Asparagus

2 to 4 servings

½ pound small asparagus,*
  ends trimmed

7 tablespoons whipping cream
  Salt and freshly ground pepper

4 eggs

Cut asparagus tips 2½ inches long; reserve for garnish. Cut stems into ½-inch pieces. Cook stems in saucepan of boiling salted water until just tender, about 2 minutes. Drain.

Bring cooked asparagus and 3 tablespoons cream to boil in heavy medium skillet, stirring constantly. Reduce heat and simmer until cream coats asparagus, about 1 minute. Season generously with salt and pepper. (*Can be prepared 1 day ahead and refrigerated.*)

Position rack in center of oven and preheat to 400°F. Butter four 6-inch shallow baking dishes or one 8 × 1-inch round dish. Heat in oven until dishes are hot, about 2 minutes.

Meanwhile, reheat asparagus mixture over medium-low heat until very hot, stirring constantly. Divide among small dishes or spread in bottom of large dish.

Break 1 egg into small bowl and then slide into dish, being careful not to break yolk; repeat, adding 1 egg to each small dish or 4 to large dish. Spoon 1 tablespoon cream over each egg. For very soft eggs, bake 5 minutes for small dishes or 6 minutes for large dish. Check and continue cooking until eggs are set.

Meanwhile, cook asparagus tips in medium saucepan of boiling salted water until just tender, about 2 minutes. Drain thoroughly. Arrange around edges of cooked eggs. Set dishes on plates and serve immediately.

*If unavailable, ³/₄ pound large asparagus can be substituted. Peel stems, cut into ¹/₂-inch pieces and cook about 4 minutes. Cook tips until just tender, about 3 minutes.

Burgundy-style Omelets with Bacon and Mushrooms

These make elegant evening or brunch fare.

6 servings

Meurette Filling
¹/₄ **pound sliced bacon, cut into ¹/₂-inch pieces**
3 **tablespoons butter**
¹/₂ **pound mushrooms, trimmed and sliced (trimmings reserved)**
1 **small onion, finely chopped**
1 **carrot, finely chopped**
1 **celery stalk, finely chopped**
1 **shallot, finely chopped**
2¹/₂ **cups dry red wine**
5 **parsley stems, tied together**
¹/₂ **bay leaf**

Pinch of dried thyme, crumbled
1 **cup whipping cream**
1 **tablespoon Dijon mustard**
1 **7-ounce can snails, drained and cut into ¹/₃-inch pieces**
¹/₄ **cup minced fresh parsley**
1 **garlic clove, minced**
Salt and freshly ground pepper

6 **tablespoons (³/₄ stick) butter**
12 **eggs**
Minced fresh parsley

For filling: Cook bacon in heavy large skillet over medium-low heat until most of fat is rendered. Transfer bacon to paper towels, using slotted spoon. Pour off all but 1 tablespoon fat in skillet. Add 2 tablespoons butter and mushrooms to skillet. Cook over medium heat until mushroom liquid evaporates, stirring frequently, about 10 minutes. Transfer mushrooms to bowl, using slotted spoon. Add 1 tablespoon butter to skillet. Add onion, carrot, celery and shallot. Reduce heat to medium-low and cook until onion is soft, stirring occasionally, about 8 minutes. Add wine, parsley stems, bay leaf, thyme and mushroom trimmings. Increase heat and simmer until reduced by half. Strain liquid and return to skillet. Add cream and simmer until reduced to ¹/₂ cup. Whisk in mustard. Stir in snails and heat through. Set aside 2 tablespoons bacon for garnish. Add remaining bacon, mushrooms, ¹/₄ cup parsley and garlic. Season sauce with salt and pepper. (*Can be prepared 4 hours ahead and refrigerated. Rewarm over low heat, stirring frequently.*)

Heat heavy 6-inch omelet pan over medium-high heat. Add 1 tablespoon butter. Beat 2 eggs to blend and add to pan. Stir eggs quickly, tilting pan to keep surface covered with egg. When eggs are almost set but still slightly creamy, remove pan from heat and place ¹/₆ of filling down center of omelet. Roll omelet onto plate, enclosing filling in center. Sprinkle with parsley and some of reserved bacon and serve. Repeat cooking with remaining butter, eggs and filling. (*Omelets can be covered loosely with foil and kept warm in 200°F oven while cooking remaining eggs.*)

🍒 A Glossary of French Cheeses

A cheese course accompanied with fresh fruit is a fundamental part of the French meal. Typically served after the main course and salad, a bite of cheese and fruit provides a soothing bridge between the savory main course and the sweet finale. It will also easily stand on its own to end a simple meal.

Almost every region produces its own type of cheese. Although some of France's finest are not exported (especially the fresh ones), many of the cheesemaking techniques and methods have been eagerly adapted here in the U.S., so it is possible to find not only imported cheeses, but delicious home-grown versions as well.

Boursin—This rich, savory cheese made from cow's milk is of the triple-cream category, which means that the cheese has at least 72 percent butterfat. With its smooth, mild flavor it can often be found embellished with such seasonings as garlic and herbs. Look for it typically packaged in foil-wrapped cylinders.

Brie—Surely the most famous of all French cheeses, Brie originates from the Ile de France region in an area east of Paris. It has been said that Charlemagne tasted its delicate creamy flavor in the year 774. Made from whole cow's milk, this delectable cheese tastes of the bounty of the French countryside, with a hint of mushrooms and a kiss of fresh fruit. The best Brie at perfect ripeness should have an even, creamy color and a smooth texture. The rind should show some discoloration around the edges and the cheese, plump within the rind, should give a little to the touch.

Camembert—Running close behind Brie in popularity, this cheese is the pride of the Normandy region. Made from cow's milk, the perfect Camembert should have a snowy white rind with a soft, supple center. Camembert, by tradition, has been packaged in thin wooden containers developed to protect the cheese during travel. Nowadays it can be found more often packaged in cardboard renditions of the original.

Chèvre—Meaning goat in French, this type of cheese is naturally made from goat's milk or a combination of goat's and cow's milk. Chèvre comes in numerous shapes, with varying texture and intensity of flavor depending

Leek and Swiss Chard Gratin

Serve this savory custard with a platter of assorted hams, pâtés and sausages accompanied by chutney, mustard, pickles and crusty bread.

12 servings

¼ cup (½ stick) butter
8 large leeks, white part only, halved and thinly sliced
1½ pounds Swiss chard, trimmed and thinly sliced
1 tablespoon fresh lemon juice
3 tablespoons minced fresh parsley

1 pound Gruyère cheese, coarsely grated
3 cups half and half
6 eggs, room temperature
¼ teaspoon salt
¼ teaspoon freshly ground white pepper
⅛ teaspoon freshly grated nutmeg

upon the region, age and tradition. Its wonderfully tart, tangy flavor is often enhanced with herbs and other seasonings. True chèvre originated in the Anjou Touraine region to the southwest of Paris. Other noteworthy types are Montrachet from the Burgundy region, a soft cheese usually formed in logs covered with chestnut or grape leaves; and Banon from Provence, which typically has a mild, milky flavor that becomes more piquant as it ages. Like Montrachet, Banon is traditionally covered in chestnut leaves.

Gruyère—Franche-Comté and the Alps, the region bordering Switzerland and Italy, is where some of the best Gruyère cheeses are produced. This type of cheese, made from a combination of whole and skimmed cow's milk, normally has a mild nutty flavor. Depending upon its age, it will be relatively dry and waxy. Gruyère, a generic term used by the French, is most notably represented by the brands Comté, Beaufort and Emmenthal.

Munster—The Alsace region in the northeast corner of France prides itself on the production of this soft cow's milk cheese, so much so that the label of origin is protected by law. The flavor ranges from mild and delicate when young, to strong and spicy when fully ripened. Variations on the classic cheese include the addition of caraway or anise seeds.

Neufchâtel—This fresh, soft cheese made with skimmed or whole cow's milk ranges in flavor from mild when young to piquant when aged a few weeks. Its consistency and flavor make it particularly suitable for use in cooking. A classic from the Normandy region, it is traditionally shaped into rounds, cylinders and heart shapes.

Port Salut—One of the most well-known cheeses from the western part of France, Port Salut has a smooth texture and mild flavor. Other brand names for this famous cow's milk cheese are St. Paulin and Bonbel. The cheese was first made in 1817 by Trappist monks, who later sold the rights to a major French cheese manufacturer—hence, its widespread availability.

Roquefort—Considered one of the great cheeses of the world, this is the only blue cheese made from goat's milk. To be called Roquefort the cheese must be cured in the caves of Mount Combalou in the Languedoc region of southwest France. Authentic Roquefort carries the red sheep emblem on its foil wrapping. At its best, Roquefort should be creamy white, with a smooth buttery texture.

Melt butter in heavy large saucepan over medium-low heat. Add leeks and cook until softened, stirring occasionally, about 10 minutes. Add chard and lemon juice and stir until chard wilts, about 5 minutes. Mix in parsley.

Position rack in center of oven and preheat to 350°F. Butter 9 × 13-inch baking dish. Spread vegetables in prepared dish. Sprinkle with cheese. Beat remaining ingredients to blend. Strain into dish. Bake 15 minutes.

Increase oven temperature to 425°F and continue baking until gratin is puffed, brown and knife inserted in center comes out clean, 20 minutes. Serve hot or at room temperature.

Eggplant and Parmesan Soufflé

4 to 6 servings

2 small eggplants (about 1 pound each), ends trimmed
2 tablespoons olive oil

16 tablespoons (1 cup) freshly grated Parmesan cheese

4 tablespoons fresh breadcrumbs
  Salt and freshly ground pepper
3 garlic cloves, minced
5 egg yolks, room temperature
6 egg whites, room temperature
  Fresh Tomato Sauce*

Preheat oven to 375°F. Cut eggplants in half. Score pulp diagonally on each half. Brush each with ½ teaspoon oil. Arrange cut side down on baking sheet. Bake until eggplant is soft but not mushy, 25 to 30 minutes. Let stand until cool enough to handle.

Preheat oven to 425°F. Brush 6-cup soufflé dish with 2 teaspoons oil. Combine 1 tablespoon Parmesan, 1 tablespoon breadcrumbs and large pinch each of salt and pepper. Coat dish with mixture. Spoon eggplant pulp into processor. Using on/off turns, mix to chunky puree. Heat remaining 2 teaspoons olive oil in heavy medium saucepan over medium heat. Add garlic and stir 30 seconds. Add eggplant puree and remaining 3 tablespoons breadcrumbs and stir until all liquid has evaporated, about 8 minutes. Whisk in yolks. Season with salt and pepper. Continue stirring until slightly thickened, 2 to 3 minutes. Add 13 tablespoons Parmesan and stir to heat through. Adjust seasoning. Using electric mixer, beat whites with pinch of salt until stiff but not dry. Stir ¼ of whites into eggplant mixture to loosen. Gently fold in remaining whites. Pour mixture into prepared dish; smooth top. Sprinkle with remaining 2 tablespoons Parmesan. Bake until puffy and golden brown, 15 to 20 minutes. Serve immediately with Fresh Tomato Sauce.

*Fresh Tomato Sauce

Makes about 1½ cups

3 large tomatoes, peeled, seeded and finely chopped
1 teaspoon fresh lemon juice
  Salt and freshly ground pepper

2 tablespoons fresh oregano, minced or 1 teaspoon dried, crumbled
1 teaspoon fresh thyme, minced or ¼ teaspoon dried, crumbled

Combine tomatoes, lemon juice and salt and pepper in colander and let stand 1 hour to drain.

Transfer tomato mixture to bowl. Stir in herbs. Serve at room temperature.

French Custard Toast

Also called Pain Perdu (literally "lost bread"), this is an ingenious way to transform day-old bread into heavenly French toast.

6 servings

12 1½-inch-thick slices day-old French bread

4 eggs, beaten to blend
4 cups extra-rich milk
⅓ cup superfine sugar
1½ tablespoons grated lemon peel
1 teaspoon vanilla

½ teaspoon salt
½ teaspoon freshly grated nutmeg

4 tablespoons (½ stick) unsalted butter
4 tablespoons vegetable oil
  Powdered sugar (garnish)
  Cane, maple or berry syrup

Arrange bread slices in single layer in two 9 × 13-inch baking dishes.

Whisk eggs, milk, sugar, lemon peel, vanilla, salt and nutmeg in large bowl until blended. Pour over bread. Let soak 5 minutes. Turn slices over. Cover dishes with plastic wrap. Refrigerate at least several hours or overnight.

Melt 2 tablespoons butter with 2 tablespoons oil on griddle or in each of two heavy large skillets (preferably non-stick) over medium-high heat. Add bread and fry until golden brown, about 5 minutes per side; do not undercook or insides will not be completely set. Transfer to heated platter. Sprinkle with powdered sugar and serve immediately. Accompany with syrup.

Goat Cheese Tart

8 servings

6 ounces mild goat cheese (such as Montrachet or Rondin de Poitou), room temperature
1/2 cup minced fresh herbs (any combination of parsley, basil, marjoram, oregano, tarragon and thyme)
1 small garlic clove, mashed
4 ounces cream cheese, room temperature

1/4 cup (1/2 stick) unsalted butter, room temperature
1/2 cup ricotta cheese, room temperature
1/3 cup crème fraîche, room temperature
2 tablespoons all purpose flour
2 jumbo eggs, room temperature
Salt and freshly ground pepper
1 9-inch Special Pie Crust,* baked

Preheat oven to 375°F. Blend goat cheese, herbs and garlic in processor until smooth, stopping occasionally to scrape down sides of work bowl. Blend in cream cheese and butter until smooth. Add ricotta cheese, crème fraîche, flour, eggs, salt and pepper and mix until smooth. Pour mixture into crust, smoothing surface. Bake until puffed and golden, about 30 minutes. Cool on rack. Serve tart warm or at room temperature.

*Special Pie Crust

Makes two 9-inch crusts

1 jumbo egg, beaten to blend
1 tablespoon cold water
2 teaspoons cider vinegar

1 2/3 cups all purpose flour
1/2 teaspoon salt

2/3 cup solid vegetable shortening, well chilled

Combine egg, water and vinegar in small bowl. Refrigerate 15 minutes.

Combine flour and salt in medium bowl. Cut in shortening until mixture resembles coarse meal. Add egg mixture and mix until just blended. Gather dough into ball. Cut in half. Wrap and refrigerate at least 10 minutes. (*Can be prepared 1 day ahead.*)

Roll one piece of dough out on lightly floured surface into 11-inch round. (Freeze remaining dough for future use.) Roll dough up on rolling pin. Unroll into 9-inch tart pan. Trim and finish edges. Refrigerate 30 minutes.

Preheat oven to 450°F. Line pastry shell with buttered foil, buttered side down. Fill with dried beans or rice. Bake until pastry is set, about 8 minutes. Remove beans and foil. Continue baking until pastry is brown, about 7 minutes. Cool on rack.

Spinach Chèvre Walnut Tart

8 servings

Quick Puff Pastry Crust
1½ cups unbleached all purpose flour
½ cup cake flour
1¾ cups (3¼ sticks) well-chilled
    unsalted butter, thinly sliced

½ teaspoon salt
¼ to ½ cup ice water

Spinach and Chèvre Filling
¾ cup whipping cream
5 ounces creamy goat cheese,
    such as Montrachet, crumbled

10 ounces fresh spinach, stemmed
1 cup boiling water

2 tablespoons (¼ stick) unsalted
    butter
¼ cup minced shallots
1 teaspoon minced garlic
½ cup chopped walnuts
    Salt
    Freshly grated nutmeg
    Cayenne pepper
2 eggs

2 tablespoons fresh breadcrumbs
1 tablespoon unsalted butter

For crust: Refrigerate both flours 4 hours. Refrigerate butter 15 minutes.

Combine both flours and salt in bowl of electric mixer. Top with butter. Using paddle attachment, beat until butter is broken into pea-size pieces and well coated with flour. Gradually mix in just enough water to bind dough (butter will still be lumpy).

Roll dough out on well-floured surface to 12 × 8-inch rectangle, sprinkling with flour if very sticky. Lightly sprinkle dough with flour. Fold in thirds as for business letter, using dough scraper as aid. Give dough quarter turn so it opens like book, lifting with scraper and flouring surface. If at any time dough contracts and becomes difficult to roll, refrigerate 30 minutes or longer as necessary. Repeat rolling, folding and turning dough 3 more times. Cover with plastic and refrigerate 1 hour.

Roll, fold and turn dough 2 more times. Wrap in plastic and refrigerate at least 20 minutes. (*Quick puff pastry can be prepared 2 days ahead.*)

Sprinkle rimless baking sheet with water. Roll dough out on floured surface to ⅛-inch-thick round. Transfer to prepared baking sheet. Press bottom of 9½-inch springform pan into center of dough, leaving indentation in dough. Remove pan. Trim dough to 1¾ inches beyond indentation. Roll edge of dough up onto indentation. Squeeze edge with fingers to form 1¼-inch-high sides. Pierce bottom of pastry with fork. Place extended sides of 9½-inch springform pan around pastry, carefully closing sides to encase. Gently press pastry against pan sides. Refrigerate at least 30 minutes to firm. (*Can be prepared up to 1 day ahead. Cover tightly with plastic wrap.*)

For filling: Stir cream and cheese in saucepan over low heat until smooth.

Reserve 8 spinach leaves for garnish. Cook remainder in saucepan of 1 cup boiling water until just wilted. Drain spinach. Squeeze dry and chop.

Melt 2 tablespoons butter in heavy small skillet over medium heat. Add shallots and garlic and cook until soft, stirring occasionally, 3 minutes. Add walnuts and stir 1 minute. Add spinach. Season with salt, nutmeg and cayenne pepper. Mix eggs into cheese mixture. Blend in spinach. (*Can be prepared 1 day ahead and refrigerated.*)

Position rack in lower third of oven and preheat to 375°F. Pour filling into cold pastry shell. Sprinkle with breadcrumbs. Dot with 1 tablespoon butter. Bake 10 minutes. Reduce temperature to 350°F and bake 10 more minutes. Remove pan edges. Continue baking tart until crust is golden brown and filling is firm to touch, covering with foil if browning too quickly, 25 to 35 minutes. Cool tart 10 minutes. Cut into 8 pieces. Place 1 reserved spinach leaf on each plate. Top with tart and serve.

4 ❦ Meat

With the exception of a few small beef-producing regions, such as the Charolais in Burgundy, meat—particularly beef—has never been plentiful in France. The thrifty household cook marinates less tender cuts of beef in wine to make a hearty *daube* or stew, such as classic Beef Stew and Vegetables with Red Wine (page 48). Expensive roasts are presented with a flavorful sauce, such as Roast Beef with Sweet Red Pepper and Zucchini Relish (page 47) and Boeuf à la Ficelle (page 46), boiled beef that is thinly sliced, topped with succulent marrow and served with a rich wine sauce and Sherry mustard.

Veal and lamb get the same delicious treatment in country dishes such as Sautéed Medallions of Veal with Garlic Cream Sauce (page 49), Veal Rolls with Chard-Morel Filling (page 50) and Marinated Lamb Roast (page 53), a garlicky favorite that is traditionally served with white beans cooked with herbs.

Throughout all of France the pig is a primary source of meat. Every part of it is used—from its snout to its tail and feet—primarily in the varied types of *charcuterie*: sausages, rillettes, hams and pâtés. Fresh pork is often cooked with fruit or chestnuts, as you will find in our flavorful Farm-style Pork with Chestnuts (page 57) and Pork Loin with Prunes (page 56). Charcuterie are used to enhance a simple dish such as Sautéed Cabbage and Apples with Smoked Garlic Sausage (page 60) or Grilled Ham Steaks with Onions and Raisins (page 58). Sausages Wrapped in Buckwheat Crepes (page 59) is a typical snack or entrée from Brittany, where crepes often take the place of bread. And Ham-stuffed Kugelhopf with Chervil and Mustard Sauce (page 57) comes straight from Alsace.

 Beef

Boeuf à la Ficelle with Marrow, Mustard and Shallot Butter

6 servings

6 cups (or more) veal or beef stock
1 3-pound center-cut beef
   tenderloin, tied to secure

¾ cup Madeira
¾ cup dry red wine
½ cup rich veal or beef stock
⅓ cup red Zinfandel vinegar or red
   wine vinegar

2 shallots, minced
1 cup (2 sticks) well-chilled
   unsalted butter, cut into
   tablespoons
   Salt and fresh white pepper

6 beef thigh marrow bones
   Sherry Mustard*

Bring 6 cups stock to simmer in heavy large saucepan. Add beef (if not completely submerged, add more stock) and simmer until meat thermometer inserted in thickest part of beef registers 120°F (for rare), about 20 minutes.

Meanwhile, boil Madeira, wine, ½ cup stock, vinegar and shallots in heavy small nonaluminum saucepan until reduced to 3 tablespoons. Remove from heat. Whisk in 2 tablespoons butter. Return to heat and whisk in butter 2 tablespoons at a time, removing pan from heat if drops of melted butter appear. Season with salt and pepper. Keep sauce warm in water bath or vacuum bottle.

Remove beef from stock. Set beef aside. Return stock to simmer. Push marrow out of bones. Cut in half crosswise. Add marrow to stock and poach 5 minutes. Drain.

Cut beef into ¼-inch-thick slices. Spoon sauce onto plates. Arrange beef atop sauce. Top with marrow. Serve immediately with mustard.

---

*Sherry Mustard

*Prepare 4 to 5 days
in advance.*

Makes about 1½ cups

1 quart water
½ cup yellow mustard seeds
¼ cup loosely packed fresh
   marjoram leaves
5 tablespoons extra-virgin olive oil
3 tablespoons Sherry wine vinegar,
   preferably 25 years old

1½ tablespoons Manzanilla Sherry
1 tablespoon fresh thyme leaves
½ teaspoon grated fresh horseradish
¼ teaspoon salt

Combine water and mustard seeds in saucepan and bring to boil. Reduce heat and simmer 15 minutes, stirring occasionally. Drain seeds; rinse under cold water until seeds are cool, then drain again. Transfer seeds to processor and puree to paste. Add remaining ingredients and blend well; mixture will not be smooth. Transfer to jar. Refrigerate until ready to serve.

Roast Beef with Sweet Red Pepper and Zucchini Relish

12 to 14 servings

1 trimmed 3-pound filet of beef
6 tablespoons vegetable oil
1/2 cup chopped onion
1/2 cup chopped carrot
1/2 cup chopped celery
2 bay leaves
10 bacon slices, blanched

Sweet Red Pepper and Zucchini Relish*
Curly endive
Red bell pepper rings
Green onion brushes

Preheat oven to 350°F. Pat meat dry. Heat oil in heavy large skillet over medium-high heat. Add meat and brown well on all sides. Transfer to rack in roasting pan. Pat vegetables onto top and sides of meat. Crumble bay leaves over. Cover vegetables with bacon. Roast meat to desired doneness, about 45 minutes for medium-rare. Discard vegetables and bacon. Cool meat completely. Cover and refrigerate until firm. (*Can be prepared up to 2 days ahead.*) Cut filet of beef diagonally into thin slices.

To serve, set bowl of relish at one end of large oval platter. Arrange meat on platter in overlapping slices. Cover edge of platter with curly endive. Top endive with pepper rings and onions.

*Sweet Red Pepper and Zucchini Relish

For maximum flavor, make this colorful condiment at least two days ahead.

Makes about 2 1/2 cups

1/4 cup olive oil
1 tablespoon minced garlic
1 1/2 cups chopped onion
1 1/2 cups chopped red bell pepper
1 1/2 cups chopped zucchini (about 2 small zucchini)

1 cup beef stock
1/2 cup Vinegar Sauce**
Salt and freshly ground pepper

Heat oil in heavy large skillet over medium heat. Add garlic and stir 30 seconds. Add onion and stir 4 minutes. Add red bell pepper and stir 3 minutes. Add zucchini and stir 3 minutes. Blend in 1/4 cup stock and 2 tablespoons Vinegar Sauce and cook until liquid evaporates. Repeat stock-sauce process 3 times. Season with salt and pepper. Cool to room temperature. Spoon into glass bowl. Chill at least 2 days. (*Can be prepared 5 days ahead.*)

**Vinegar Sauce

Makes 1/2 cup

1/2 cup water
1/4 teaspoon ground allspice
1/8 teaspoon dried red pepper flakes

1 bay leaf
1/4 cup balsamic vinegar

Bring water, allspice, pepper flakes and bay leaf to boil in nonaluminum small saucepan. Reduce heat and simmer 5 minutes. Add vinegar and simmer 5 minutes. Discard bay leaf. (*Can be prepared 5 days ahead. Cool completely and refrigerate in airtight jar.*)

Beef Stew and Vegetables with Red Wine

4 servings

2 tablespoons vegetable oil
1 tablespoon butter
2 pounds boneless beef chuck, trimmed, patted dry and cut into 1¼- to 1½-inch pieces
1 large onion, chopped
1 tablespoon plus 1 teaspoon all purpose flour

1¼ cups dry red wine
1¾ to 2¼ cups beef stock
6 parsley stems
1 medium garlic clove, minced
1 fresh thyme sprig or ½ teaspoon dried, crumbled

1 bay leaf
Salt and freshly ground pepper
8 ounces thin carrots, peeled and cut into 1-inch pieces

6 ounces small white onions (unpeeled)
1 tablespoon butter
1 small fennel bulb, stalks discarded, diced (optional)
1 pound fresh peas, shelled or 1 cup frozen
2 tablespoons minced fresh parsley

Position rack in lower third of oven and preheat to 450°F. Heat oil and 1 tablespoon butter in heavy 4- to 5-quart flameproof casserole over medium-high heat. Add ⅓ of beef and brown on all sides, making sure pieces do not touch, 6 to 7 minutes. Transfer beef to plate using slotted spoon. Repeat with remaining beef. Add chopped onion to pan, reduce heat to low and cook until translucent, stirring often, about 7 minutes. Return beef to pan; reserve any juices on plate. Sprinkle beef with flour. Toss gently until well coated. Transfer to oven and bake uncovered, stirring once, 5 minutes. Remove from oven.

Reduce oven temperature to 325°F. Pour reserved juices from plate over beef. Add wine and then enough stock to barely cover. Tie parsley stems, garlic, thyme and bay leaf in cheesecloth. Add to beef with salt and pepper. Bring mixture to boil on top of stove, scraping any browned bits from sides and bottom of pan. Transfer to oven, cover and bake, stirring occasionally, 45 minutes. Stir in carrots. Add more stock if mixture appears dry or sauce is too thick. Continue baking until carrots are tender when pierced with tip of sharp knife, 30 to 45 minutes. Discard cheesecloth bag.

Meanwhile, bring medium saucepan of water to boil. Add onions and boil 1 minute. Drain; rinse under cold water. Peel onions. Melt 1 tablespoon butter in heavy medium skillet over medium heat. Add onions and sauté until lightly browned, about 4 minutes. Remove onions using slotted spoon; transfer to stew in oven. Add fennel if desired. Continue baking 20 minutes. Sauce should be thick enough to lightly coat back of spoon. If sauce is too thick, stir in additional stock. If sauce is too thin, transfer stew to top of stove, uncover and carefully remove beef and vegetables using slotted spoon. Boil sauce, stirring often, until slightly thickened. Return beef and vegetables to sauce. (*Can be prepared 3 days ahead, covered and refrigerated or 1 month ahead and frozen.*) Add peas and simmer until all vegetables are tender, 5 to 10 minutes. Stir in minced parsley. Adjust seasoning. Serve stew hot.

Veal

Veal Scallops with Morels

2 servings

½ **pound fresh morels***

2 **tablespoons (¼ stick) unsalted butter**
1 **tablespoon vegetable oil**
1 **tablespoon minced shallot**

10 **ounces veal scallops**
   All purpose flour

¼ **cup Marsala or Madeira**
¼ **cup beef broth**
½ **cup crème fraîche or whipping cream**
   Salt and freshly ground pepper
   Minced fresh parsley

Rinse morels under water until all sand is removed. Drain well; pat dry. Slice larger morels if desired.

Melt 1 tablespoon butter with oil in heavy large skillet over medium heat. Add morels and stir 2 minutes. Add shallot and stir 2 minutes. Transfer to bowl. Do not rinse skillet.

Pound veal to thickness of ⅛ to 1/16 inch. Dredge in flour, shaking off excess. Melt remaining butter in same skillet over medium-high heat. Add veal and brown quickly on both sides. Add Marsala and broth and bring to boil. Reduce heat and cook until veal is tender, about 2 minutes. Transfer veal to plates; keep warm. Add crème fraîche to skillet and boil until thick and syrupy. Add morel mixture and heat through. Season generously with salt and pepper. Spoon sauce over veal. Sprinkle with parsley and serve.

*If unavailable, 1 ounce dried morels can be substituted. Soak in lukewarm water until soft and spongy, about 1 hour.

Sautéed Medallions of Veal with Garlic Cream Sauce

Just-cooked spinach and wild mushrooms are served with this simple yet sophisticated main course.

6 servings

12 **large garlic cloves**
14 **tablespoons (1¾ sticks) unsalted butter**
¾ **pound wild mushrooms (such as cèpes, morels, shiitake or oyster), sliced if large**

2¼ **pounds veal tenderloin, cut crosswise into 18 pieces**
   Salt and freshly ground pepper
1¼ **cups rich veal stock**
½ **cup whipping cream**

¾ **pound spinach, stemmed and blanched**

Preheat oven to 450°F. Wrap 6 unpeeled garlic cloves in foil. Roast until very soft, about 40 minutes.

Peel remaining 6 garlic cloves. Blanch 30 seconds in boiling water. Repeat twice. Set blanched garlic aside.

Melt 4 tablespoons butter in heavy large skillet over medium heat. Add mushrooms and stir until softened, 4 to 5 minutes. Set aside.

Pat veal dry. Season with salt and pepper. Melt 6 tablespoons butter in heavy large skillet over medium-high heat. Add veal and sear quickly in batches on both sides; reduce heat and continue cooking until meat is cooked through but still rare. Remove from skillet. Pour off fat. Stir in stock, scraping up browned bits.

Add blanched garlic and boil until liquid is reduced to 1 cup. Puree mixture in blender. Return to skillet. Add cream and boil until reduced to 1 cup. Reduce heat to low. Whisk in 4 tablespoons butter 1 tablespoon at a time. Season with salt and freshly ground pepper.

Add blanched spinach to sautéed mushrooms and stir to heat through.

Ladle sauce onto plates. Top with 3 slices of veal. Mound vegetables at side. Top with roasted garlic clove.

Sautéed Veal Chops Stuffed with Chèvre and Dill

Ask the butcher to cut chops with two- to three-inch-long bones and the meat to one side of the bone.

6 servings

6 ³/₄-inch-thick veal rib chops, trimmed
8 ounces goat cheese (preferably Montrachet)
2 tablespoons minced fresh dill or 2 teaspoons dried dillweed
1¹/₂ teaspoons grated lemon peel
¹/₂ teaspoon coarsely ground pepper

1 cup milk
1 egg, beaten to blend
1¹/₃ cups dry breadcrumbs
³/₄ cup all purpose flour
Salt and freshly ground pepper
Vegetable oil
6 thin lemon slices
6 dill sprigs

Freeze chops until firm but not solid, to facilitate cutting. Place chop on work surface. Hold knife parallel to surface and cut deep, wide pocket in center of chop. Repeat with remaining chops. Mix goat cheese, minced dill, lemon peel and ¹/₂ teaspoon pepper. Spread 2 tablespoons mixture in pocket of each chop. Secure with toothpicks. (*Can be prepared 6 hours ahead. Cover and refrigerate.*)

Mix milk and egg in pie pan. Spread breadcrumbs on one plate and flour on another. Season veal with salt and pepper. Dip in flour; shake off excess. Dip in milk mixture, then roll in breadcrumbs; shake off excess. Heat ¹/₈-inch-deep layer oil in 2 heavy large skillets over medium heat. Add chops and cook until crisp on outside and just pink in center, 4 to 5 minutes per side. Arrange in pairs on heated platter, crossing bones. Top with lemon slices and dill sprigs and serve.

Veal Rolls with Chard-Morel Filling

6 to 8 servings

1 4-pound boned veal breast, butterflied, halved lengthwise and trimmed (bones and trimmings reserved)

Veal Stock
2 medium carrots
1 medium celery stalk
1 bouquet garni (parsley, thyme, bay leaf)
1 teaspoon salt
¹/₄ teaspoon dried thyme, crumbled

Chard-Morel Filling
1 ounce dried morels
1¹/₂ cups warm water

1¹/₄ pounds green Swiss chard,* trimmed of white stems

4 tablespoons (¹/₂ stick) butter
1 small onion, thinly sliced
¹/₂ cup crème fraîche
Salt and freshly ground pepper

3 tablespoons butter
1 tablespoon olive oil
2 medium carrots, sliced
1 medium onion, sliced

For stock: Boil veal bones and trimmings with stock ingredients and water to cover in large saucepan 1 hour. Strain liquid into saucepan. Boil until reduced to 2 cups; degrease.

For filling: Soak morels in warm water 1 hour. Drain, reserving liquid. Rinse morels and squeeze dry, reserving liquid. Chop finely, discarding hard core, and squeeze dry, reserving liquid. Strain liquid through sieve lined with dampened paper towels.

Boil chard in several quarts of rapidly boiling salted water 3 minutes. Drain, squeeze dry and chop finely.

Melt 2 tablespoons butter in heavy large skillet over medium heat. Add onion and cook until translucent, stirring occasionally, about 10 minutes. Add chard, crème fraîche, salt and pepper and stir until crème thickens enough to coat chard. Puree mixture in processor. Melt another 2 tablespoons butter in same skillet over medium heat. Stir in morels and ¼ cup morel liquid. Increase heat and boil until liquid has almost evaporated. Add salt and pepper. Blend chard and morel mixtures.

Spread thin layer of filling over each veal half, leaving 1-inch border; do not overfill. Roll up starting from pointed end. Trim, tuck or sew ends. Tie rolls at 1-inch intervals. Pat dry.

Preheat oven to 400°F. Melt butter with oil in heavy large skillet over medium heat. Brown veal on all sides, about 20 minutes. Transfer to 6-quart Dutch oven. Add carrots and onion to same skillet and stir 5 minutes. Transfer vegetables and fat to Dutch oven. Pour stock into skillet, scraping up any browned bits. Add to Dutch oven. Salt veal lightly. Cover and oven-braise until rolls are tender (knife should pierce meat easily), about 70 minutes, basting every 15 minutes.

Rest veal on carving board 30 minutes. Meanwhile, degrease pan juices. Strain juices into heavy small saucepan. Boil until sauce is reduced to 1 cup. Adjust seasoning. Discard strings from veal. Cut into slices using string indentations as guide. Arrange 2 slices on each plate. Top with sauce and serve.

*If unavailable, spinach can be substituted.

Roasted Loin of Veal with Three Vegetables

Zucchini, summer squash and carrots are cut into thin noodlelike strands and tossed with fresh pasta to make four-colored "spaghetti."

8 to 10 servings

Pasta
- 2 cups unbleached all purpose flour
- 3 eggs
- 2 egg yolks
- ½ teaspoon salt
  Additional unbleached all purpose flour

- 3 large zucchini
- 3 large yellow summer squash
- 2 large carrots, peeled

Sauce
- 1 tablespoon unsalted butter
- ½ pound veal stew meat, cut into 1-inch cubes
- 1 quart veal stock
- 1 tablespoon minced fresh savory or 1 teaspoon dried, crumbled

Veal
- 1 6-pound veal loin, boned, rolled and tied at ½-inch intervals
- ½ cup (1 stick) butter, melted
- ½ cup dry breadcrumbs
- 2 teaspoons minced fresh savory or ⅔ teaspoon dried, crumbled

- 4 tablespoons (½ stick) butter
- 2 medium shallots, minced
- 1 large garlic clove, minced

- 2 tablespoons minced fresh parsley
  Salt and freshly ground pepper

- 6 tablespoons (¾ stick) unsalted butter, room temperature
  Watercress sprigs (garnish)

For pasta: Arrange 2 cups flour in mound on work surface or in large bowl and make well in center. Add eggs, yolks and salt to well and blend with fork. Gradually draw flour from inner edge of well into center until all flour is incorporated. Lightly flour work surface and hands. Knead dough until no air bubbles are visible when cut in half, about 20 minutes, kneading in additional flour as necessary. Cover with inverted bowl and let rest for at least 15 minutes.

Cut pasta into 4 pieces. While working 1 piece, keep remaining dough covered. Flatten piece of dough with heel of hand, then fold in thirds. Turn pasta machine to widest setting and run dough through several times until smooth and velvety (number of times will depend on how vigorously dough was kneaded by hand). Adjust pasta machine to next narrower setting. Run dough through machine, dusting lightly with flour if sticky. Repeat, narrowing rollers after each run until pasta is $1/16$ inch thick. Hang dough sheet on drying rack or set on kitchen towels. Repeat with remaining dough. Set aside until sheets look firm and leathery and edges begin to curl but are not brittle, 10 to 30 minutes, depending on dampness of dough and temperature of kitchen. *Pasta must be cut at this point or dough will be too brittle.*

Run dough sheets through narrowest blades of pasta machine or slice into $1/8$-inch-wide noodles by hand. Arrange pasta on kitchen towel or drying rack, overlapping as little as possible. Set aside until ready to cook.

Peel zucchini and yellow squash in long strips. (Reserve pulp for another use.) Cut peels lengthwise into $1/8$-inch-wide strands. Transfer to bowl and cover with plastic. Cut carrots lengthwise into $1/16$-inch-wide slices. Cut slices lengthwise into $1/8$-inch-wide strands. Blanch carrots 1 minute in boiling salted water to cover. Rinse with cold water and drain. Cool completely. Mix with zucchini and yellow squash. Cover and set aside.

For sauce: Heat 1 tablespoon butter in heavy large saucepan over medium-high heat. Pat veal stew meat dry. Add to pan and brown on all sides. Add stock and boil until liquid is reduced to $1\frac{1}{2}$ cups, about 30 minutes. Strain stock through fine sieve into clean saucepan. (Reserve veal for another use.) Whisk savory into stock.

For veal: Preheat oven to 400°F. Brush veal loin generously with melted butter. Mix breadcrumbs and 2 teaspoons savory on piece of waxed paper. Roll veal in mixture, coating evenly. Set on rack in roasting pan. Roast until thermometer inserted in thickest portion of meat registers 130°F, about 40 minutes. Let stand 5 minutes.

Meanwhile, melt 2 tablespoons butter in heavy large skillet over medium-low heat. Add shallots and garlic and cook until just beginning to color, about 5 minutes. Add vegetable strands and stir until crisp-tender, about 1 minute.

Bring large amount of salted water to rapid boil in large pot. Add pasta and stir vigorously to prevent sticking. Cook until just firm but almost tender to the bite (al dente), about 2 minutes. Drain well. Return pasta to pot. Rewarm vegetables over high heat and toss with pasta. Stir in 2 tablespoons butter, parsley, salt and pepper. Cover.

Quickly slice veal $1/4$ to $1/2$ inch thick and arrange on serving platter. Season with salt and pepper. Gently rewarm sauce and whisk in 6 tablespoons butter, 1 tablespoon at a time. Spoon several tablespoons over meat. Surround meat with vegetable-pasta mixture. Garnish with watercress sprigs. Serve immediately. Pass sauce separately.

 # *Lamb*

Marinated Lamb Roast

The lamb is presented very rare in the French manner. Adjust roasting time to suit your own taste. Serve it with White Beans with Tomatoes and Herbs (see page 82).

8 servings

2 large garlic cloves
½ cup dry red wine
¼ cup Sherry wine vinegar
¼ cup olive oil
1 teaspoon dried oregano, crumbled

1 teaspoon salt
1 4½-pound leg of lamb (sirloin end), boned

1½ teaspoons salt
Freshly ground pepper

Insert steel knife in processor. With machine running, drop garlic through feed tube and mince finely. Add wine, vinegar, oil, oregano and 1 teaspoon salt and blend 3 seconds. Transfer to large plastic bag. Add lamb and seal airtight. Refrigerate 1½ to 2 days, turning bag occasionally.

Bring lamb to room temperature. Position rack in center of oven and preheat to 500°F. Pat lamb dry. Sprinkle with 1½ teaspoons salt and pepper. Place in shallow roasting pan. Roast until thermometer inserted in thickest part of lamb registers 125°F for very rare, about 25 minutes. Remove lamb from oven. Tent with foil and let stand 20 minutes. Slice meat across grain. Arrange slices on platter and serve.

Loin of Lamb with Red Wine, Onion and Rosemary

An easy-to-prepare company dish.

8 servings

Red Wine and Onion Sauce
3 tablespoons unsalted butter
2 cups chopped red onion
1 cup dry red wine
4 medium garlic cloves, minced

2 cups Rich Lamb Stock*
2 teaspoons minced fresh rosemary
1 teaspoon cracked black pepper
½ teaspoon salt

2 tablespoons olive oil
2 1⅓-pound boned lamb loin eyes, well trimmed and tied to hold shape

8 rosemary sprigs

For sauce: Melt butter in heavy medium saucepan over medium heat. Add onion and cook until translucent, stirring occasionally, about 5 minutes. Add wine and garlic. Reduce heat and simmer until wine evaporates completely, stirring frequently, about 10 minutes. Puree mixture in processor.

Simmer stock in heavy medium saucepan until reduced to ½ cup, about 10 minutes. Add onion puree. Simmer until mixture coats spoon, about 5 minutes. Strain into heavy small saucepan. Mix in minced rosemary, cracked black pepper and salt.

Position rack in lower third of oven and preheat to 400°F. Heat oil in heavy ovenproof skillet over high heat. Add lamb and brown on all sides, about 5 minutes. Transfer skillet to oven. Cook lamb until thermometer inserted in thickest part registers 130°F for rare, about 10 minutes. Transfer to platter. Let rest 5 minutes.

Remove string and halve each lamb loin crosswise, then cut lengthwise into

1/4-inch-thick slices. Reheat sauce. Spoon some onto plates. Arrange lamb across sauce. Top each serving with 1 teaspoon of sauce. Garnish with rosemary. Pass any remaining sauce separately.

*Rich Lamb Stock

Makes 1¹/₂ quarts

1 pound lamb bones
1 pound veal bones
2 cups coarsely chopped onion
1 cup peeled and coarsely chopped carrot

1 bunch parsley stems
2 tablespoons black peppercorns
1 tablespoon fresh thyme
2 bay leaves

Rinse bones under cold water. Place in heavy 8-quart pot. Cover with water. Bring to boil, skimming surface. Add all remaining ingredients. Reduce heat and simmer 24 hours, adding water as necessary to keep bones submerged. Degrease stock. Strain into clean pot. Boil until reduced to 1¹/₂ quarts. (*Can be prepared 5 days ahead and refrigerated.*)

Stuffed Breast of Lamb

Serve this elegant roast with whipped potatoes seasoned with garlic and cheese.

8 servings

Chard Stuffing
1 pound chard, celery cabbage or kale (hard stems removed), cut into 1-inch pieces
2 leeks (green part only), cut into 1-inch pieces
4 ounces pork stew meat, cut into 1-inch pieces
1 bunch parsley, stems removed
1 small onion, quartered
2 slices bread, soaked in ¹/₃ cup milk 5 minutes

1 large garlic clove
2 eggs
Salt and freshly ground pepper

7 pounds breast of lamb (2 or 3 pieces), boned
1 pound sliced bacon

³/₄ cup dry white wine
1 quart lamb or veal stock

For stuffing: Finely chop first 7 ingredients in processor. Add eggs, salt and pepper and blend well.

Arrange lamb cut side up on work surface, overlapping short ends slightly. Spread stuffing over lamb leaving 1-inch border. Roll lamb up jelly roll fashion, starting at 1 long side. Wrap with bacon. Tie with kitchen twine to hold shape. Transfer to roasting pan.

Preheat oven to 450°F. Roast lamb 45 minutes. Add wine to pan and scrape up any browned bits. Pour in stock. Turn lamb over. Cover pan with foil. Continue roasting 1 hour.

Transfer lamb to platter and let stand 10 minutes. Degrease pan juices. Slice lamb and arrange on plates. Spoon pan juices over and serve.

Pork

Pork Tenderloin Sauté with Gratin of Turnips

Accompany this elegant dish with rice seasoned with a generous quantity of chopped green onion.

4 servings

Gratin of Turnips
- 3 tablespoons clarified butter
- 2 1/2 pounds young turnips, peeled and cut into 1/4-inch rounds
- 2 medium onions, chopped
- 2 tablespoons minced fresh parsley Salt and freshly ground pepper
- 1 cup dry vermouth
- 3 cups meat or poultry stock (preferably homemade)

- 1/4 teaspoon sugar Pinch of cinnamon

Tenderloin Sauté
- 2 1-pound pork tenderloins, trimmed of all fat
- 3 tablespoons clarified butter Salt and freshly ground pepper

- 4 1/2 tablespoons minced shallots
- 1/4 cup Cognac
- 1 1/3 cups dry red wine
- 1 teaspoon minced fresh tarragon or 1/3 teaspoon dried, crumbled Pinch of dried thyme, crumbled
- 3 cups meat or poultry stock (preferably homemade)
- 1 1/2 teaspoons red wine vinegar
- 1 1/2 teaspoons tomato paste
- 1 1/2 tablespoons minced cornichons
- 1 1/2 teaspoons water-packed green peppercorns, rinsed, drained and crushed
- 2 tablespoons minced fresh parsley

For turnips: Grease 12-inch gratin dish. Heat butter in heavy large skillet over medium-high heat. Sauté turnips 3 minutes; add onions and sauté until golden, about 7 minutes. Mix in parsley and sauté 30 seconds. Sprinkle with salt and pepper. Pour in vermouth and boil until liquid is reduced to glaze, scraping up any browned bits, about 4 minutes. Add stock and boil until reduced by half. Reduce heat and simmer until turnips are just tender, about 15 minutes. Increase heat and boil until liquid is reduced to 1/2 cup, about 12 minutes. Transfer to gratin dish. Cool to room temperature. (*Can be prepared 1 day ahead to this point. Cover and refrigerate. Bring to room temperature before continuing.*)

Preheat oven to 375°F. Bake turnips 10 minutes. Sprinkle with sugar and cinnamon and continue baking 15 minutes. (*Can be kept warm in oven on lowest setting for 20 minutes.*)

Meanwhile, prepare tenderloin: Cut each tenderloin into 5 slices, 1 1/2 inches thick at wide end of tenderloin and slightly thicker as meat narrows. Flatten each to 1-inch thickness, using heel of hand. Shape into rounds and pat dry. Heat butter in heavy large skillet over medium-high heat. Brown tenderloin pieces on all sides, including edges. Reduce heat to medium-low. Cook meat 6 minutes. Turn and cook second side until cooked through, about 6 more minutes. Transfer to heated platter and sprinkle with salt and pepper. Tent with foil.

Pour off all but 3 tablespoons fat from skillet. Add shallots and stir over medium-high heat 1 minute. Pour in Cognac and boil until reduced to glaze. Stir in 2/3 cup wine, tarragon and thyme. Boil until reduced to glaze, scraping up any browned bits, about 2 minutes. Add remaining 2/3 cup wine and boil until reduced to glaze. Mix in stock, vinegar and tomato paste. Boil, stirring occasionally, until sauce is thickened and reduced by 3/4, about 15 minutes. Stir in cornichons, green peppercorns, salt and pepper. Divide pork and turnips among heated dinner plates. Nap meat with sauce. Sprinkle with parsley and serve.

Pork Chops Baked with Chestnuts, Mushrooms and Onions

6 servings

18 chestnuts*

9 tablespoons corn oil
3 medium onions, halved and cut into ¼-inch-thick slices
¼ teaspoon sugar
6 ¾-inch-thick center-cut pork chops, trimmed

Salt and freshly ground pepper
All purpose flour
2½ cups (or more) beef stock (preferably homemade)
6 ounces mushrooms, quartered

Cut X on one side of each chestnut. Cook in medium saucepan of boiling water 4 minutes. Turn off heat. Remove 3 chestnuts at a time and peel off outer shell and inner peel. Halve chestnuts lengthwise.

Preheat oven to 350°F. Heat 5 tablespoons oil in heavy large ovenproof skillet over medium heat. Add onions and cook until beginning to brown, stirring frequently, about 15 minutes. Add sugar and cook until onions are very brown, stirring frequently, about 10 minutes. Drain on paper towels. Discard pan drippings; wipe skillet clean. Pat pork chops dry. Sprinkle with salt and pepper. Dredge in flour. Heat 4 tablespoons oil in same skillet over medium-high heat. Add pork (in batches if necessary; do not crowd) and cook until brown, about 5 minutes per side. Discard pan drippings. Return chops to skillet. Add 2½ cups stock. Distribute chestnuts, onions and mushrooms over pork chops. Bring liquid to simmer. Cover skillet with foil and lid. Bake until pork is very tender, about 45 minutes, adding more stock to skillet if all liquid evaporates. Transfer to heated platter.

*Canned unsweetened chestnuts can be substituted. Do not blanch in boiling water.

Pork Loin with Prunes

8 servings

4 dozen dried pitted prunes
4 cups semidry, fruity white wine (such as Vouvray)

Vegetable oil
2 pork tenderloin fillets (about 1 pound each), cut into 1½-inch slices and retied to retain shape
¼ cup (½ stick) butter

¼ cup diced carrot
¼ cup diced celery
¼ cup diced onion

2 cups whipping cream
¼ cup crème de cassis
Salt and freshly ground pepper
2 tablespoons minced fresh parsley

Soak prunes in wine at least 2 hours. Drain, reserving wine.

Heat thin layer of oil in heavy deep skillet over medium-high heat. Pat pork dry. Add to skillet and brown well on all sides. Remove from skillet. Melt butter in same skillet over medium-high heat. Add vegetables and cook until lightly browned, stirring frequently, about 10 minutes. Stir in wine, scraping up browned bits. Add pork. Reduce heat to low. Cover and simmer gently until pork is tender, 10 to 15 minutes; do not overcook.

Transfer pork to platter. Tent with foil to keep warm. Strain pan juices, pressing on vegetables to extract as much liquid as possible. Stir juices back into skillet, scraping up browned bits. Boil until reduced to ½ cup. Add cream and boil until reduced to 1½ cups. Add prunes and crème de cassis and heat through. Season with salt and pepper. Remove foil from pork. Arrange prunes atop pork. Spoon sauce over. Sprinkle with parsley.

Salad of Vodka-marinated Tomato and Green Beans; Apple and Root Vegetable Soup; Rich Rice Pudding with Poached Pears and Marmalade Sauce

Irwin Horowitz

Burgundy-style Omelets with Bacon and Mushrooms; Pepper Seed Thin Breads; Ragout of Dried Fruits; steamed asparagus (recipe not included); Champagne punch (recipe not included)

Mediterranean Potato Salad with Mussels and Shrimp

Irwin Horowitz

Clockwise from bottom left: Trout Mousse with Mushroom Sauce; Green Herb Soup with Polenta Garnish; Wilted Spinach and Lettuce Salad

Clockwise from bottom left: Cauliflower Soup with Cinnamon; Walnut Bread; Fruit Salad with Bachelor's Confit; Roast Chicken with Garlic Croutons; Carrot, Pea and Salsify Sauté

Farm-style Pork with Chestnuts

6 servings

2 pounds chestnuts

1³/₄ pounds pork tenderloin, trimmed, fat reserved
Salt and freshly ground pepper

1¹/₂ cups dry red wine

1¹/₂ cups rich veal stock

4 medium onions, cut in eighths

1 carrot, halved lengthwise and cut into ¹/₂-inch chunks

2 large garlic cloves, crushed

2 leeks, cut into ¹/₂-inch rounds

Pierce each chestnut using sharp knife. Cover chestnuts with cold water in large saucepan and bring to boil. Remove from heat. Remove chestnuts from water 1 at a time and peel off outer and inner skins. If chestnuts become hard to peel, return water to boil, then continue peeling. Steam peeled chestnuts 15 minutes.

Pat pork dry. Melt reserved pork fat in heavy large skillet over medium-high heat. Add pork and brown well on all sides. Sprinkle with salt and pepper. Add wine, stock, onions, carrot and garlic and bring to simmer. Cover and cook 30 minutes, adjusting heat so cooking liquid is barely shaking.

Add chestnuts and leeks to pork. Continue cooking until instant-reading thermometer inserted in pork registers 170°F and vegetables are tender, about 30 minutes; do not overcook.

Strain liquid into heavy medium saucepan. Boil liquid until reduced to thin saucelike consistency; degrease. Return to vegetables. Slice pork and arrange around platter. Spoon vegetables and sauce into center and serve.

Ham-stuffed Kugelhopf with Chervil and Mustard Sauce

A traditional Alsatian recipe that makes a stunning centerpiece for a buffet.

8 to 10 servings

Bread Dough

1¹/₂ envelopes dry yeast

1 teaspoon sugar

¹/₂ cup warm milk (105°F to 115°F)

3 cups sifted all purpose flour (or more)

1 teaspoon salt

2 eggs, room temperature

¹/₂ cup (1 stick) unsalted butter, cut into 8 pieces, room temperature

Stuffing

1 pound ground pork shoulder

4 medium shallots, minced

1 large garlic clove, minced

³/₄ pound ground ham

¹/₄ cup minced fresh chervil or ¹/₄ cup minced fresh parsley and 2 teaspoons dried chervil, crumbled

¹/₄ teaspoon quatre épices*

¹/₈ teaspoon freshly ground pepper

2 eggs, beaten to blend

Chervil and Mustard Sauce**

For dough: Sprinkle yeast and sugar onto warm milk; stir to dissolve. Let stand until bubbly, about 10 minutes.

Combine 3 cups flour and salt in bowl of electric mixer fitted with dough hook. Add yeast and eggs and mix until well combined, about 4 minutes. Stir in butter 1 piece at a time, beating until well blended, about 2 minutes. Mix in additional flour if necessary to form slightly sticky, elastic dough. Knead on lightly floured surface until smooth, about 2 minutes. Warm large bowl with hot water. Dry bowl; grease with butter. Add dough, turning to coat entire surface. Cover with towel. Let rise in warm draft-free area until doubled, 1³/₄ hours.

For stuffing: Lightly brown pork in heavy large skillet over medium heat, stirring constantly. Add shallots and garlic and cook until soft and golden, stirring frequently, about 5 minutes. Mix in ham, chervil, quatre épices and pepper. Cool to room temperature.

Generously butter 9-inch bundt pan. Punch dough down. Knead on lightly floured surface until smooth and elastic, about 3 minutes. Cover and let rest on heavily floured surface 5 minutes. Roll ²/₃ of dough out on lightly floured surface to 6 × 20-inch oval. Gently fit into prepared pan, pressing up sides and center tube to 1 inch from top. Press ends together to seal. Mix eggs into stuffing and spoon mixture into pan, packing lightly. Roll remaining dough out on lightly floured surface to 4 × 20-inch oval. Arrange on top of filling, pinching ends together to seal. Fold dough lining pan over top and pinch edges to seal. Cover pan with towel. Let dough rise in warm draft-free area 45 minutes.

Position rack in center of oven and preheat to 400°F. Bake kugelhopf until golden brown, 35 to 40 minutes.

Run thin-bladed knife between bread and pan. Invert onto plate. Let rest 10 minutes. Serve with sauce.

* Available at specialty foods stores.

**Chervil and Mustard Sauce

Makes about 1³/₄ cups

½ cup Alsatian Riesling, Sylvaner or other dry white wine	⅓ cup minced fresh chervil or ¼ cup minced fresh parsley and 1½ teaspoons dried chervil, crumbled
½ cup whipping cream	
⅓ cup crème fraîche	
1 cup (2 sticks) chilled unsalted butter, cut into 16 pieces	3 tablespoons Alsatian or Dijon mustard

Boil wine in heavy small saucepan over medium heat until reduced to glaze, about 10 minutes. Add cream and crème fraîche. Boil until reduced by half, whisking constantly. Remove from heat and whisk in 2 pieces butter. Set pan over low heat and whisk in remaining butter 1 piece at a time, removing pan from heat briefly if drops of melted butter appear. (If sauce breaks down at any time, remove from heat and whisk in 2 pieces cold butter.) Remove from heat and blend in chervil and mustard. Serve immediately.

Grilled Ham Steaks with Onions and Raisins

A simple slice of ham is turned into something special in this recipe.

6 servings

6 ⅓-inch-thick slices fully cooked smoked ham	Pinch of sugar Salt and freshly ground pepper
1 quart milk, chilled	
⅓ cup raisins, rinsed in warm water	2 cups rich veal stock, preferably homemade
3 tablespoons marc de Champagne,* Cognac, Armagnac or brandy	6 cornichons, thinly sliced 1 to 2 tablespoons Dijon mustard
4 tablespoons (½ stick) butter	Vegetable oil
1 pound pearl onions, parboiled and peeled	Minced fresh parsley
1 cup Chardonnay or dry white wine	12 green onions, cut decoratively

Place ham in large baking dish. Cover with milk. Let stand at room temperature 2 hours; turn ham occasionally.

Combine raisins and marc in medium bowl. Let stand 2 hours.

Melt 2 tablespoons butter in heavy large skillet over medium-high heat. Add onions and cook until well browned, stirring frequently, 8 to 9 minutes. Stir in wine, sugar and salt and pepper. Reduce heat and simmer until onions are tender and liquid is reduced to glaze, 12 to 13 minutes. Mix glazed onions into raisins.

Stir stock into skillet, scraping up browned bits. Boil until reduced to about 1⅓ cups. Whisk 2 tablespoons butter into boiling stock. Remove from heat. Add onion mixture and cornichons. Whisk in mustard. Adjust seasoning. Keep sauce warm in water bath or over very low heat.

Drain ham; pat dry. Heat grill or heavy large cast-iron skillet over medium-high heat. Brush lightly with oil. Add ham and sear well on both sides. Reduce heat and cook until heated through. Arrange ham on platter. Spoon sauce over. Sprinkle with parsley. Garnish with green onions.

*Spirit distilled from grape skins, pulp and seeds that remain after the wine has been pressed out. Available at liquor stores.

Sausages Wrapped in Buckwheat Crepes

Serve these sausages with hard cider.

Makes 18 to 20

Sausages

1½ pounds pork butt, trimmed and cut into 1-inch cubes
½ pound fresh unsalted pork fatback, cut into 1-inch cubes
¼ pound slab bacon (rind removed), cut into 1-inch cubes
2 chicken livers, cut into 1-inch pieces
3 large shallots, minced
2 medium garlic cloves, crushed
2 tablespoons applejack
1 tablespoon freshly ground pepper
1½ teaspoons ground coriander seed
½ teaspoon finely ground fennel seed
¼ teaspoon dried thyme, crumbled

Salt
10 feet sausage casing,* rinsed inside and out

Buckwheat Crepes

2 tablespoons currants
2 tablespoons applejack

1 cup buckwheat flour**
1½ tablespoons all purpose flour
2 eggs
1 tablespoon brown sugar
¼ teaspoon salt
¼ teaspoon Quatre Epices***
1⅔ cups milk
5 tablespoons corn oil

Vegetable oil

1 cup water
Apple slices (optional garnish)

For sausages: Place first 4 ingredients in glass bowl. Mix in shallots, garlic, applejack, pepper, coriander, fennel and thyme. Marinate in refrigerator 24 hours, stirring occasionally.

Grind meat mixture with coarse blade of meat grinder. Mix in salt. To check seasoning, fry small piece of mixture until cooked through. Taste, then adjust seasoning of uncooked portion if necessary. Fit meat grinder or heavy-duty mixer with sausage horn. Squeeze all water from sausage casing. Tie knot at 1 end. Pull casing over horn until knot touches tip. Grind sausage mixture directly into casing. (Casing can also be stuffed using pastry bag or funnel with ¾- to 1-inch opening.) Tie end of casing. Twist and tie sausage at 3½- to 4-inch intervals; cut apart.

For crepes: Soak currants in applejack at least 1 hour, stirring occasionally.

Mix buckwheat flour, all purpose flour, eggs, sugar, salt and Quatre Epices in large bowl. Gradually add milk, stirring until smooth. Blend in oil. Let batter rest 30 minutes.

Mince currants and add to batter with soaking liquid. Heat 7-inch crepe pan or heavy skillet over medium-high heat. Grease with paper towels soaked in oil. Remove fron heat. Working quickly, add about 3 tablespoons batter to pan, tilting until bottom is covered with thin layer of batter. Pour any excess batter back into bowl. Cook crepe until bottom is lightly browned, loosening edges with knife. Turn crepe over and cook second side. Slide onto plate. Repeat with remaining batter, oiling pan as necessary. (*Crepes can be prepared 1 day ahead and refrigerated. Wrap in foil and reheat in 350°F oven for about 15 minutes.*)

Pour 1 cup water into large skillet. Prick sausages and add to skillet. Bring to simmer and cook, turning occasionally, until sausages have rendered fat and browned on both sides, about 25 minutes. Drain on paper towels. Wrap each sausage in 1 crepe. Garnish with apple slices if desired and serve.

*Sausage casing is available at specialty markets and butcher supply stores.
**Available at natural foods stores.

***Quatre Epices

Makes about 3 tablespoons

2 **teaspoons ground allspice**	1 **teaspoon freshly grated nutmeg**
2 **teaspoons ground coriander**	1/2 **teaspoon ground cardamom**
2 **teaspoons dried tarragon**	1/2 **teaspoon dried marjoram**
1 **teaspoon cinnamon**	1/8 **teaspoon ground cloves**

Mix all ingredients in blender at high speed until finely powdered.

Sautéed Cabbage and Apples with Smoked Garlic Sausage

4 servings

2 **small onions, halved**	1/4 **cup firmly packed light brown sugar**
1½ **tablespoons vegetable oil**	1/4 **cup cider vinegar**
1 **pound green cabbage, cut into wedges to fit feed tube**	1 **teaspoon dried thyme, crumbled**
3 **small tart red apples, halved lengthwise and cored**	1 **teaspoon salt**
1 **pound smoked garlic sausage (such as kielbasa), cut into 1/2-inch-thick slices**	**Freshly ground pepper**

Slice onions in food processor with medium slicer. Heat oil in heavy 12-inch skillet over medium-low heat. Add onions and cook until soft and translucent, stirring frequently, about 8 minutes.

Arrange cabbage wedges cut side down in feed tube and slice using firm pressure. Add to onions. Carefully remove medium slicer and insert thick slicer.

Stand apples in feed tube and slice using medium pressure. Add to onions. Mix in remaining ingredients. Increase heat to medium-high, cover and cook until cabbage just begins to soften, stirring occasionally, about 4 minutes. Taste and adjust seasoning. Transfer to bowl using slotted spoon. Serve immediately.

5 ❦ Poultry and Game

A fixture in any farmyard, chickens are an essential part of French country life, from the succulent, plump-breasted birds of Bresse, to the more common hens that provide eggs and meat for the family table. Whether they're specially fattened capons for a holiday feast or older birds that are slowly stewed with wine to make them more tender, chickens are cooked with care and finesse. Our sampling of recipes includes fragrant Roast Chicken with Garlic Croutons (page 62) and an easy, classic Coq au Vin (page 63). Chicken is sautéed in beer for an Alsatian favorite (page 63), and pot-roasted with candied onions and asparagus for extra flavor (page 65) in Brittany.

Geese and ducks are as pervasive as chickens on the French country scene—and even more treasured. Especially prized duckling in Brittany and Normandy are breeds created by crossing wild and domestic varieties. And down south in the Périgord, the famous force-fed geese give their livers for the treasured foie gras. We include two dishes that you can prepare here, using, in French fashion, every part of the bird: Duck Leg, Radish and Zucchini Ragout (page 69) and Grilled Duck Fillets with Juniper Berries (page 68).

Game birds such as squab, pheasant and partridge have, until modern times, been very plentiful and popular in France. Rabbit is still a favorite and, as it is becoming more readily available in the U.S., we include two great ways of preparing it: Normandy Rabbit in Cider (page 71) and Sauté Rabbit Chasseur (page 72).

Roast Chicken with Garlic Croutons

4 servings

1 3-pound chicken, neck and giblets reserved
  Salt and freshly ground pepper
5½ ounces day-old French bread, cut into 1½ × 1½-inch croutons
3 large garlic cloves, halved

2 to 3 fresh thyme sprigs or ½ teaspoon dried, crumbled

2 tablespoons (¼ stick) butter
1 tablespoon vegetable oil
  Fresh thyme sprigs

Pat chicken dry. Sprinkle cavity with salt and pepper. Rub croutons on all sides with garlic. Place 2 to 3 croutons and thyme in cavity. Truss chicken to hold shape. Sprinkle outside with salt and freshly ground pepper.

Position rack in center of oven and preheat to 375°F. Melt butter with oil in roasting pan over medium-high heat. Add chicken and brown well on all sides. Set chicken breast side up and roast 24 minutes. Add remaining croutons, neck and giblets to pan and roast until juices run clear when thigh is pierced with fork, about 12 minutes. Transfer chicken to platter. Garnish with thyme. Pass garlic croutons seperately.

Roast Chicken with Wild Mushrooms

8 servings

2 3½-pound chickens
  Salt and freshly ground pepper
8 tablespoons (or more) butter
2 tablespoons olive oil
1 cup dry white wine

1 pound fresh morels, cèpes, shiitake or combination,* stemmed, caps cut into matchstick julienne

2 tablespoons Cognac

Sprinkle insides of chickens with salt and pepper. Truss chickens to hold shape. Melt 2 tablespoons butter with 1 tablespoon olive oil in each of 2 heavy large skillets over medium-high heat. Pat chickens dry and brown on all sides (do not tear skin). Transfer chickens to roasting pan breast side up. Discard fat from skillets. Add ½ cup wine to each and boil 30 seconds, scraping up browned bits. Pour into pan (do not pour over chickens).

Position rack in center of oven and preheat to 375°F. Sprinkle chickens with salt and pepper. Roast until drumsticks move easily in sockets and juices run clear when flesh is pierced, about 65 minutes, basting frequently with pan juices and adding water to pan to maintain 1½ cups liquid.

Melt remaining 4 tablespoons butter in heavy large skillet over medium-high heat. Add mushroom julienne and stir 2 minutes. Season with salt and pepper. Reduce heat to medium-low, cover and braise 15 minutes, stirring mushrooms occasionally, adding more butter to skillet if necessary.

Heat Cognac in heavy small saucepan. Pour 1 tablespoon over each chicken and ignite. When flames subside, transfer to cutting board and carve each into 8 pieces. Degrease juices in roasting pan. Pour any exuded chicken juices back into pan. Bring to boil. Stir in mushrooms. Adjust seasoning. Arrange 2 pieces of chicken on each plate. Spoon some of sauce over and serve immediately.

*If fresh are unavailable, 6 ounces dried can be substituted. Soak in warm water 30 minutes before using. Baste chicken with mushroom soaking liquid instead of water.

Chicken Sautéed in Beer Alsatian Style

Delicious with buttered egg noodles and sautéed fresh mushrooms.

4 servings

1 4-pound chicken, cut into serving pieces
  Salt and freshly ground pepper
3 tablespoons butter
1 large onion, chopped
1 large garlic clove, minced
1 large bay leaf
2 whole cloves
3 cups beer (do not use dark)

1 tablespoon butter
1 tablespoon all purpose flour
1 cup whipping cream
  Pinch of freshly grated nutmeg
3 egg yolks, beaten to blend

Pat chicken dry. Season with salt and pepper. Melt 3 tablespoons butter in heavy deep skillet over medium-high heat. Add chicken and cook on both sides until golden brown. Add onion, garlic, bay leaf and cloves. Pour in beer. Reduce heat, cover and simmer gently until legs are tender when pierced with fork, 20 to 25 minutes. Remove chicken and keep warm. Boil sauce 5 minutes. Strain.

Melt 1 tablespoon butter in heavy medium saucepan over low heat. Whisk in flour and cook 3 minutes. Gradually whisk in strained liquid and bring to boil. Add cream and nutmeg and bring to boil. Ladle a little liquid into yolks and blend well. Whisk mixture back into pan and cook until heated through; do not boil or sauce will curdle. Pour over chicken and serve.

Coq au Vin

4 to 6 servings

6 bacon slices, chopped
4 whole chicken breasts, split
1 teaspoon salt
¼ teaspoon freshly ground pepper
¼ cup brandy
2 cups dry white wine
1 cup chicken broth
1 garlic clove, minced
1 bay leaf

3 tablespoons butter
6 small onions, peeled and quartered
½ pound mushrooms, quartered
¼ cup all purpose flour
2 tablespoons (¼ stick) butter, melted
  Fresh parsley sprigs
  Freshly cooked rice

Cook bacon in heavy large skillet over medium heat until done but not crisp, about 8 minutes. Remove with slotted spoon. Add chicken to same skillet and cook until browned, about 6 minutes per side. Season with salt and pepper. Return bacon to skillet. Pour brandy into pan and heat briefly; ignite with match. When flames subside, add wine, broth, garlic and bay leaf. Reduce heat, cover and simmer 30 minutes.

Meanwhile, melt 3 tablespoons butter in heavy medium skillet over medium heat. Add onions and mushrooms and cook until softened, stirring occasionally, about 6 minutes. Add to chicken. Discard bay leaf. Mix flour and 2 tablespoons melted butter in small bowl until paste forms. Stir into chicken and simmer until sauce thickens. Transfer to serving platter. Garnish with parsley sprigs. Serve chicken immediately with rice.

Chicken Braised with Triple Onions

In this French entrée, chicken is cooked with onions, leeks and garlic, then served with pearl onions.

6 to 8 servings

2 3-pound chickens, cut into serving pieces
Salt and freshly ground pepper

¼ cup olive oil
1½ cups dry white vermouth

¼ cup (½ stick) unsalted butter
½ pound leeks, white part only, thinly sliced
10 ounces onions, thinly sliced

24 large garlic cloves, blanched 3 minutes
2 tablespoons fresh thyme leaves or 2 teaspoons dried, crumbled
2 tablespoons fresh lemon juice
2 teaspoons grated lemon peel

Caramelized Onions*
12 to 16 homemade 3½-inch heart-shaped croutons
Fresh thyme sprigs

Pat chicken dry. Season generously with salt and pepper. Let stand 15 minutes at room temperature.

Heat oil in heavy large skillet over medium-high heat. Add chicken and brown in batches on both sides until just golden. Remove to ovenproof baking dish. Pour off all but 2 tablespoons fat from skillet. Stir in ½ cup vermouth, scraping up browned bits. Boil until syrupy. Pour over chicken.

Melt butter in same skillet over medium-low heat. Add leeks, onion and garlic and cook until softened and just beginning to color, stirring occasionally, about 15 minutes. Add thyme leaves and stir 2 minutes. Add lemon juice and peel and stir 2 minutes. Scatter over chicken. Stir remaining 1 cup vermouth into skillet, scraping up browned bits, and boil until reduced to ⅓ cup. Pour over chicken. (*Can be prepared 2 to 3 hours ahead.*)

Position rack in center of oven and preheat to 375°F. Cover chicken loosely with parchment (do not tuck in sides). Bake until chicken is golden brown and juices run clear when thigh is pierced, 30 to 40 minutes. Let stand 20 minutes at room temperature.

To serve, arrange chicken on plates. Surround with onion mixture and Caramelized Onions. Spoon pan juices over chicken. Garnish with heart-shaped croutons and thyme sprigs.

*Caramelized Onions

Makes about 4 cups

2 tablespoons (¼ stick) unsalted butter
1½ tablespoons olive oil
1½ pounds pearl onions, blanched and peeled
3 tablespoons sugar

¼ cup Sherry vinegar or white wine vinegar
⅓ cup dried currants, rinsed and drained
¼ cup dry Sherry or dry white wine
Salt

Melt butter with olive oil in heavy large skillet over medium-low heat. Add onions. Sprinkle with sugar. Cook until onions are softened and light golden brown, stirring frequently, about 30 minutes. Increase heat to high. Stir in vinegar and cook until liquid is reduced by half. Reduce heat to medium-low. Add currants and toss 3 minutes. Add Sherry and pinch of salt and cook until onions are caramelized and juices are syrupy, stirring occasionally, about 10 minutes. Cool to lukewarm before serving.

Pot-roasted Chicken with Candied Onions and Asparagus

4 servings

4 tablespoons (¹/₂ stick)
  unsalted butter
2 pounds white onions, halved and
  thinly sliced (root ends reserved)

¹/₂ pound asparagus, peeled

1 4-pound chicken
  Salt and freshly ground pepper
2 tablespoons cider vinegar

1 cup veal stock
  Watercress (garnish)

Melt 2 tablespoons butter in heavy large skillet over medium-low heat. Add onions; cover and cook 10 minutes, stirring occasionally. Uncover and cook until deep brown, about 45 minutes, increasing heat to medium during last 5 minutes if necessary.

Blanch asparagus in large amount of boiling salted water until crisp-tender. Rinse with cold water and drain. Cut diagonally into 1¹/₂-inch pieces.

Season cavity of chicken with salt and pepper; add reserved onion roots. Truss chicken. Melt remaining 2 tablespoons butter in heavy casserole over medium-high heat. Add chicken and brown well. Season with salt and pepper. Add vinegar to pan, reduce heat to low and cover tightly. Cook until juices run clear when chicken is pricked with fork, turning and basting once or twice, about 55 minutes.

Transfer chicken to warm platter. Add veal stock to pan and bring to boil over high heat. Simmer until reduced to saucelike consistency. Degrease sauce. Pour half of sauce into gravy boat. Add onions to pan. Reduce heat, cover and simmer until onions are hot, about 5 minutes. Add asparagus to pan and simmer until just hot. Arrange vegetables around chicken. Garnish with watercress and serve immediately. Pass sauce separately.

Chicken Niçoise Style

6 servings

2 3- to 3¹/₂-pound chickens, cut into
  6 pieces each
3 tablespoons fresh lemon juice
1¹/₂ teaspoons dried thyme, crumbled
  Salt

11 tablespoons olive oil
¹/₂ cup unpitted Niçoise olives

2 medium leeks, white part only,
  thinly sliced
1 large onion, thinly sliced
2¹/₂ ounces lean salt pork, rinsed and
  coarsely chopped
2 large garlic cloves, minced

2 bay leaves
¹/₂ teaspoon fennel seed,
  coarsely crushed

²/₃ cup dry white wine or vermouth

6 large, firm, ripe tomatoes,
  quartered and drained briefly on
  paper towels
  Freshly ground pepper

²/₃ cup fresh white breadcrumbs

¹/₃ cup minced fresh parsley

Arrange chicken in single layer in baking dish. Sprinkle with lemon juice, thyme and salt. Marinate chicken 20 minutes at room temperature.

Pat chicken dry. Heat 3 tablespoons olive oil in heavy large skillet over medium-high heat. Brown chicken in batches on both sides until pale golden. Return chicken to baking dish. Tuck Niçoise olives between chicken pieces. Pour off fat from skillet.

Heat 4 tablespoons olive oil in same skillet over medium heat. Add leeks, onion and salt pork and cook until vegetables just begin to color, stirring occasionally, about 10 minutes. Add garlic, bay leaves and fennel and stir 3 minutes. Remove with slotted spoon and spread over chicken.

Stir in white wine or vermouth and boil until liquid is reduced to ⅓ cup. Pour over chicken.

Heat 2 tablespoons olive oil in same skillet over medium-high heat. Add tomatoes, season with salt and pepper and sauté until partially cooked and liquid evaporates, 3 to 4 minutes per side. Arrange tomatoes over chicken.

Heat remaining 2 tablespoons olive oil in heavy small skillet over medium-high heat. Add breadcrumbs and stir until golden. Sprinkle over chicken.

Position rack in center of oven and preheat to 375°F. Roast chicken until golden brown, 30 to 40 minutes. Let stand 20 minutes. Garnish with fresh parsley and serve immediately.

Fricassée of Chicken Legs in Gamay

6 servings

1 750-ml bottle Gamay
  or Beaujolais
2 medium onions, thinly sliced
3 medium shallots, thinly sliced
1 carrot, thinly sliced
4 garlic cloves, thinly sliced
12 juniper berries, crushed
1 teaspoon dried marjoram, crumbled
  Bouquet garni (thyme, parsley, bay leaf)
4 tablespoons (or more) grappa,* marc,* applejack or other brandy
6 chicken legs with thighs attached

6 tart green apples, peeled, cored, halved and thickly sliced
1 cup seedless red grapes, preferably peeled

½ cup (1 stick) butter
1½ teaspoons unsweetened cocoa powder
1 tablespoon all purpose flour
  Brown veal stock, preferably homemade

  Sugar

2 tablespoons sour cream, room temperature
  Additional grappa, marc, applejack or other brandy
  Fresh lemon juice
  Salt and freshly ground pepper
  Minced fresh parsley
  Butter-fried croutons (optional)

Bring wine, onions, shallots, carrot, garlic, juniper berries, marjoram and bouquet garni to boil in heavy large saucepan. Reduce heat and simmer gently until reduced by ¼, about 20 minutes. Cool completely. Blend in 2 tablespoons brandy. Arrange chicken in single layer in large glass dish. Pour marinade over. Cover and refrigerate 2 to 4 days, turning occasionally.

Combine apples with 1 tablespoon brandy in bowl. Mix grapes with 1 tablespoon brandy in another bowl. Marinate at room temperature 2 hours.

Remove chicken from marinade (reserve vegetables and liquid) and pat dry. Melt ¼ cup butter in heavy large skillet over medium-high heat. Brown chicken well on both sides. Remove from skillet. Transfer vegetables from marinade to skillet (discard bouquet garni) and stir-fry until brown. Reduce heat to medium-low. Whisk in cocoa powder and flour and stir 3 minutes. Meanwhile, heat marinade in nonaluminum saucepan. Stir into skillet. Add chicken and enough stock to cover. Increase heat to high and bring to boil. Reduce heat, cover partially and simmer until juices run yellow when thigh is pierced, 25 minutes.

Meanwhile, melt remaining ¹/₄ cup butter in heavy large skillet over medium-high heat. Add apples and sprinkle lightly with sugar. Turn apples over and cook until browned and slightly caramelized, about 10 minutes. Sprinkle lightly with sugar. Turn apples again and cook 10 minutes; do not overcook or apples will be mushy. Transfer to prepared plate. Do not wash skillet. Arrange chicken and apples on platter. Cover with foil.

Strain marinade into same skillet. Boil until reduced to 1¹/₄ cups. Reduce heat and whisk in sour cream (do not boil or sauce will curdle). Season to taste with brandy, lemon juice, salt and pepper. Stir in grapes and heat slightly. Pour sauce over chicken. Sprinkle with parsley. Garnish with croutons if desired. Serve immediately.

*Grappa (Italy) and marc (France) are brandies distilled from grape pomace.

Braised Cornish Hens with Apple, Potato and Turnip Stuffing

An elegant light entrée.

6 servings

12 ounces baking potatoes

1³/₄ cups chicken broth
14 ounces turnips, peeled and cut into ¹/₂-inch cubes
1 7-ounce Golden Delicious apple, peeled and cut into ¹/₂-inch cubes
¹/₂ teaspoon dried marjoram, crumbled
¹/₄ teaspoon dried thyme, crumbled
¹/₄ teaspoon freshly grated nutmeg
¹/₈ teaspoon dried rosemary, crumbled

1 teaspoon unsalted butter
1 teaspoon salt
¹/₈ teaspoon freshly ground pepper

3 1-pound Cornish game hens
2 tablespoons clarified butter
¹/₄ cup Calvados, applejack or brandy
¹/₂ cup unsweetened apple juice

Red- and green-skinned apple wedges
Watercress

Position rack in center of oven and preheat to 425°F. Bake potatoes until tender, about 45 minutes.

Meanwhile, combine 1 cup broth with next 6 ingredients in heavy medium saucepan. Cover and simmer until turnips and apple are tender, about 30 minutes. Drain off any liquid and reserve. Halve potatoes and scoop flesh into saucepan with turnip mixture. Mash to lumpy texture. Mix in 1 teaspoon butter, salt and pepper. Cool completely. Maintain oven at 425°F.

Stuff turnip mixture into cavities of hens. Skewer and lace closed. Truss hens to hold shape. Heat clarified butter in heavy large skillet over high heat. Pat hens dry. Add to skillet and brown on all sides, 6 to 8 minutes. Transfer hens to platter. Pour Calvados into skillet. Boil until reduced to rich brown glaze, scraping up any browned bits, about 20 seconds. Mix in remaining ³/₄ cup broth, apple juice and any liquid reserved from turnips. Boil until thickened slightly, 4 to 5 minutes. Return hens to skillet, breast side up. Baste generously with pan liquid. Bake until hens are tender when pierced with fork, basting every 10 minutes, about 30 minutes.

Cool hens 15 minutes, basting frequently with pan drippings. Remove pins and string. Split each hen lengthwise. Transfer to heated platter. Garnish with apple wedges and watercress.

Sausage-stuffed Squabs with Apples and Calvados

6 servings

1 pound bulk pork sausage
1 egg, beaten to blend
$^{1}/_{2}$ cup chopped onion
2 tablespoons finely chopped fresh parsley
2 garlic cloves, minced

6 12-ounce squabs
  Salt and freshly ground pepper

6 bacon slices, halved
$^{1}/_{2}$ cup (or more) butter, melted

2 medium apples, peeled, cored and cut into $^{1}/_{4}$-inch-thick slices
6 $^{1}/_{2}$-inch-thick slices home-style white bread or brioche
$^{1}/_{4}$ cup Calvados

Cook sausage in heavy medium skillet over medium heat until no longer pink, breaking up with spoon, about 3 minutes. Drain and cool slightly. Combine sausage, egg, onion, parsley and garlic in bowl. Cool completely.

Preheat oven to 425°F. Pat squabs dry. Season inside and out with salt and pepper. Stuff with sausage mixture. Close openings with poultry pins and lace with kitchen string. Arrange breast side up on rack in roasting pan. Cover breast of each squab with bacon. Brush squab with $^{1}/_{4}$ cup melted butter. Roast until juices run clear when pierced in thigh, basting often, about 30 minutes.

Meanwhile, heat remaining $^{1}/_{4}$ cup melted butter in heavy large skillet over medium heat. Add apple slices and sauté until golden brown, about 3 minutes. Remove with slotted spoon. Add bread to skillet and cook until brown, adding more melted butter if necessary, about 1 minute per side. Drain on paper towels. Transfer to platter. Arrange apple slices on bread. Top each with squab. Heat Calvados in heavy small saucepan over low heat and ignite with match. Spoon flaming Calvados over each squab and serve.

Grilled Duck Fillets with Juniper Berries

French cooks are known for their thriftiness and the following three recipes illustrate the point perfectly. No part of the duck is wasted: The breast fillets are used in this recipe, the legs in another, and the carcasses and wings make a richly flavored stock.

6 servings

6 duck breast fillets, skinned, trimmed and patted dry (see Duck Stock, page 69)

1$^{1}/_{2}$ tablespoons vegetable oil
20 juniper berries, crushed to fine powder

6 tablespoons ($^{3}/_{4}$ stick) unsalted butter, room temperature

1 tablespoon green Chartreuse liqueur
$^{1}/_{2}$ teaspoon coarsely cracked mixed black and white peppercorns
$^{1}/_{8}$ teaspoon finely grated lemon peel
  Salt

$^{1}/_{4}$ cup fresh orange juice
  Watercress bouquets

Arrange duck fillets in baking dish. Brush both sides lightly with oil and sprinkle with some of juniper. Let stand at room temperature 2 hours.

Set butter in bowl. With blade of large knife work in remaining juniper, Chartreuse, peppercorns, lemon peel and pinch of salt. Let stand at room temperature 1 hour. Shape butter into cylinder. Wrap in plastic. Chill 1 hour.

Heat ribbed grill pan* over medium-high heat. Season fillets generously with salt. Grill 2 to 3 minutes on each side, pressing down with tight-fitting lid after turning onto second side. Transfer to plates. Deglaze grill with half of orange juice. Deglaze again with remaining orange juice. Divide butter evenly among fillets. Pour small amount of orange glaze over butter. Garnish with watercress and serve.

*A heavy stovetop pan that is ridged across the cooking surface. If unavailable, a barbecue grill or broiler can be used.

Duck Stock

Makes about 4¹/₂ quarts

3 5-pound fatty ducks
4 medium onions
3 leeks, dark green leaves trimmed
2 small carrots

Large bouquet garni (parsley, thyme, bay leaf)
1 envelope unflavored gelatin
1 chicken bouillon cube

Preheat oven to 400°F. Detach leg and thigh in one piece from ducks by severing above ball joint. Reserve for Duck Leg, Radish and Zucchini Ragout. Using slim sharp knife, scrape along rib cage to release breast fillets. Reserve for Grilled Duck Fillets with Juniper Berries. Chop carcasses. Arrange pieces in large roasting pan. Roast 45 minutes, turning occasionally. Transfer to stockpot. Drain fat from pan. Deglaze with hot water, stirring to scrape up browned bits. Strain into stockpot. Add remaining ingredients. Add enough water to cover ingredients by 1 inch. Bring to boil over medium heat, skimming as necessary. Reduce heat and simmer until reduced to 3 cups, about 4 hours. Strain. Cover and chill. Discard fat before using.

Duck Leg, Radish and Zucchini Ragout

6 servings

6 duck legs with thighs attached
   Salt and freshly ground pepper
¹/₄ teaspoon ground allspice

²/₃ cup dry vermouth
3 tablespoons apple cider vinegar
1 teaspoon tomato paste
¹/₂ teaspoon meat extract

5 tablespoons butter
1 medium onion, thickly sliced
2 medium shallots, thickly sliced
1 small carrot, thickly sliced
3 garlic cloves, crushed
   Bouquet garni (parsley, thyme, bay leaf)
   Duck Stock (see above)

1 bunch radishes, sliced
   ¹/₆ inch thick
3 small zucchini, sliced
   ¹/₆ inch thick

1 tablespoon all purpose flour
   Salt

   Minced fresh parsley
6 butter-fried croutons (optional)

Preheat oven to 325°F. Season duck legs with salt, pepper and allspice. Arrange skin side up on rack set in large roasting pan. Roast 1 hour.

Set duck aside. Retain oven temperature. Discard fat from pan. Stir in vermouth to deglaze pan. Blend in 2 tablespoons apple cider vinegar, tomato paste and meat extract.

Melt 2 tablespoons butter in heavy large saucepan over medium heat. Add onion, shallots, carrot and garlic and stir until barely browned, about 5 minutes. Top with duck and bouquet garni. Add vermouth mixture and enough stock to just cover duck. Bring to boil. Press piece of foil (dull side up) on top of meat and up sides of pan, then cover tightly. Return to oven and braise until juices run yellow when thigh is pierced, about 1 hour.

Meanwhile, melt 1 tablespoon butter in heavy large skillet over high heat. Add radishes and remaining 1 tablespoon vinegar and stir 3 minutes. Remove from skillet; dry skillet. Add 1 tablespoon butter. Reduce heat to medium, add zucchini and stir until translucent, about 3 minutes.

Strain duck cooking liquid and degrease. If necessary to accentuate flavors, reduce over high heat in small pan to no less than 1 cup. Blend flour with remaining 1 tablespoon butter until smooth. Whisk into reduced liquid and bring to boil. Reduce heat to medium and cook 2 minutes. Season sauce with salt if necessary.

Remove skin from duck if desired. Add radishes and zucchini to duck. Strain sauce over. Rewarm quickly over high heat. Garnish with parsley and croutons and serve immediately.

Game and Pistachio Sausages

This delicious sausage should be made at least one day ahead.

6 servings

1 pound skinned, boned and trimmed red poultry or game meat (such as duck, quail, pigeon), bones reserved

6 eggs, room temperature

10 feet sausage casings*

2 tablespoons crumbled dried cloud ear mushrooms**

6 tablespoons (3/4 stick) unsalted butter

1 1/2 teaspoons salt

1 teaspoon freshly ground pepper

1 1/4 cups whipping cream

1 tablespoon unsalted butter

1/4 cup peeled husked pistachios (2 ounces in shells)

1 1/2 cups red wine from Champagne province, Pinot Rouge d'Alsace or Pinot Noir

1/2 cup freshly squeezed red grape juice

1 tablespoon red wine vinegar

3 shallots, finely chopped

1 tablespoon crumbled dried cloud ear mushrooms

1 1/2 teaspoons quatre épices***
Bouquet garni (parsley stems, bay leaf, thyme)

2 tablespoons (1/4 stick) unsalted butter

4 cups rich veal stock, preferably homemade

3 tablespoons peeled husked pistachios (1 1/2 ounces in shells)

3 tablespoons chilled unsalted butter

1 1/2 tablespoons sour cream
Fresh lemon juice

1/4 cup (1/2 stick) butter

6 grape leaves, rinsed

Puree meat and eggs in processor until smooth, scraping bowl often, about 5 minutes. Transfer to bowl. Cover with plastic wrap and refrigerate 2 hours.

Wash salt off casings by slipping one end over faucet and running warm water through. Set casings aside.

Soak 2 tablespoons mushrooms in hot water to cover until soft, 30 minutes.

Cream 6 tablespoons butter in processor until white and fluffy. Add salt and pepper. Blend in chilled meat mixture in batches. With machine running, pour 1 cup cream through feed tube in thin stream. Transfer mousse to bowl. Cover and refrigerate. Chill remaining 1/4 cup cream.

Drain mushrooms and pat dry; cut out hard core. Melt 1 tablespoon butter in heavy small skillet over medium-high heat. Add mushrooms and sauté 2 minutes. Cool completely.

Pour remaining 1/4 cup cream over mousse. Sprinkle with 1/3 of sautéed mushrooms and 1/4 cup pistachios. Fold until mixture is homogenous. Refrigerate until well chilled.

Tie knot at one end of casing. Spoon mousse into pastry bag fitted with 1/2-inch plain tip. Push all of casing over tip so knot is at center. Pipe mousse into casing until completely filled (stop occasionally to mold meat; do not pack too full or sausage will burst as filling expands during cooking). Tie knot at other end. To form individual sausages, knot string around sausages at 3-inch intervals or twist 1 measured link clockwise and next one counter-clockwise to prevent unwinding. Sausage can also be shaped using stuffing horn of heavy-duty mixer. (*Can be prepared 1 day ahead and refrigerated.*)

Combine sausages in large pot with enough cold water to cover. Slowly bring water to 200°F (just below boiling point) and poach sausages until just firm, turning occasionally, about 20 minutes. Cool completely in poaching water. Chill in water 24 hours.

Combine wine, grape juice, vinegar, shallots, 1 tablespoon mushrooms, quatre épices and bouquet garni in saucepan and boil until reduced to ½ cup; strain and set aside.

Melt 2 tablespoons butter in heavy deep saucepan over medium-high heat. Add reserved bones and brown well. Pour off butter. Add 1 cup stock to pan and boil until reduced to 3 tablespoons. Add another 1 cup stock and boil until reduced to ½ cup. Add 1 cup stock and boil until reduced to ¾ cup. Add 1 cup stock and boil until reduced to 1 cup. Strain into reduced wine mixture. Simmer 5 minutes to blend flavors. (*Can be prepared 1 day ahead, covered and refrigerated. Reheat gently before using.*) Mix in remaining sautéed mushrooms and 3 tablespoons pistachios. Whisk in 3 tablespoons butter and sour cream. Adjust seasoning with lemon juice, salt and pepper.

Peel skins off sausages. Melt ¼ cup butter in heavy large skillet. Add sausages and sauté until golden brown on all sides. Arrange grape leaves on platter. Top with sausages. Spoon sauce over and serve immediately.

*Available at specialty foods markets and butcher supply stores.
**Available at oriental markets.
***Available at specialty foods markets.

Normandy Rabbit in Cider

4 servings

1 tablespoon unsalted butter
1 tablespoon vegetable oil
1 2½-pound rabbit, cut into
   6 pieces, patted dry
2 medium onions, cut in eighths
2 medium carrots, diced
4 cups unsweetened apple cider
3 thyme sprigs or ½ teaspoon
   dried, crumbled

2 bay leaves
4 whole black peppercorns

4 tart apples, peeled, cored
   and quartered
¼ cup minced fresh parsley

Melt butter with oil in heavy large skillet over medium-high heat. Add rabbit and brown quickly on all sides. Remove from skillet. Add onions and carrots and stir until lightly browned, about 5 minutes. Add cider, thyme, bay leaves and peppercorns and bring to simmer. Add rabbit. Cover and cook until tender, stirring occasionally and adjusting heat so liquid is barely shaking, 25 minutes.

Remove rabbit from skillet. Boil liquid in skillet until reduced by half, 20 to 30 minutes. Reduce heat to medium. Add apples and cook until just tender, about 10 minutes. Return rabbit to skillet; heat through. Top with parsley.

Sauté Rabbit Chasseur

6 servings

6 tablespoons vegetable oil
4 large carrots, diced
1 large onion, diced

1 quart canned whole Italian tomatoes (undrained)
12 shallots, peeled
12 large mushrooms, halved
6 tarragon sprigs
6 bay leaves
2 teaspoons salt

½ teaspoon freshly ground pepper
½ teaspoon ground cloves

2 tablespoons (¼ stick) butter
2 3½-pound rabbits, cut into serving pieces
All purpose flour
6 large garlic cloves, peeled
2 cups dry white wine
3 cups rich veal or chicken stock
1 tablespoon tomato puree

Heat 4 tablespoons oil in heavy large skillet over medium-low heat. Add carrots and onion and cook until onion is translucent, stirring often, about 10 minutes. Transfer to roasting pan using slotted spoon.

Drain tomatoes, reserving half of liquid. Puree tomatoes. Spread over carrot mixture in roasting pan. Add reserved liquid, shallots, mushrooms, tarragon, bay leaves, salt, pepper and cloves to pan.

Preheat oven to 350°F. Melt butter with remaining oil in heavy large skillet over medium heat. Pat rabbit dry. Dredge in flour, shaking off excess. Add to skillet (in batches; do not crowd) and brown well on one side. Turn rabbit over. Add garlic to skillet. Brown rabbit well on second side. Transfer rabbit and garlic to roasting pan. Pour off fat from skillet. Set over high heat. Stir in wine, scraping up browned bits, and bring to boil. Add stock and 1 tablespoon tomato puree and boil until sauce is slightly thickened. Pour over rabbit. Cover pan with aluminum foil. Bake until rabbit is tender when pierced with knife, about 1 hour. Serve immediately.

6 ❦ Fish and Shellfish

The French enjoy an abundance of fish and shellfish. From the chilly waters of the English Channel come herring, turbot, halibut, monkfish, mullet and the incomparable Dover sole, as well as mussels, oysters, scallops and lobster. Along the sunny Mediterranean, they harvest similar varieties of seafood, as well as sea bass, sardines, tuna, anchovies, clams and spiny *langoustes*. In Bordeaux, on the Atlantic, you can find sturgeon, skate, eel, shad, oysters, prawns and lobster. Inland, there are countless rivers and lakes providing freshwater fish such as trout, pike, salmon, eel, carp and perch.

This bounty from local waters is prepared in many different ways, from Grilled Red Snapper Saint-Malo (page 74), served with a mustard and anchovy hollandaise, to a southern-style Sea Bass with Pistou Sauce (page 76) and classic Trout Forestière (page 77), with mushrooms, green onions and wine. There's an easy Baked Fillet of Salmon with Mustard-glazed Cucumbers (page 74) and an equally simple Turbot with Lemon and Herbs (page 77) and a platter of steamed seafood served with a Basil and Mint Pistou (page 79).

Grilled Red Snapper Saint-Malo

The French province of Brittany, famous for its seafood, inspired this recipe. It can also be made with cod.

4 servings

½ pound tomatoes, peeled, seeded and coarsely chopped
4½ teaspoons vegetable oil
4 teaspoons snipped fresh chives
½ teaspoon white wine vinegar
   Salt and freshly ground pepper

Mustard and Anchovy Hollandaise
½ cup dry white wine
2 shallots, minced

3 egg yolks, room temperature

¾ cup (1½ sticks) unsalted butter, melted and cooled to lukewarm
1 tablespoon Dijon mustard
2 teaspoons anchovy paste

1½ pounds red snapper fillets, small bones removed

1 large cauliflower, separated into florets and cooked until tender

Drain tomatoes in colander 15 minutes, tossing occasionally.

Mix tomatoes, 1½ teaspoons vegetable oil, 1 teaspoon chives, vinegar, salt and pepper in small bowl. Let stand at room temperature until ready to use or up to 2 hours.

For hollandaise: Combine wine, shallots and pinch of pepper in heavy small saucepan and boil until reduced to 3 tablespoons. Cool slightly.

Whisk yolks into wine reduction. Set pan over low heat and whisk until mixture is creamy and slowly dissolving ribbon forms when whisk is lifted, about 4 minutes. (Do not allow pan to get too hot or mixture will curdle.) Remove pan from heat. Whisk mixture 30 seconds. Whisk in butter 1 drop at a time until sauce has absorbed 2 to 3 tablespoons. Whisk in remaining butter in thin stream. Whisk in mustard, anchovy paste and pinch of pepper. Adjust seasoning. Keep sauce warm in water bath or vacuum bottle.

Preheat broiler or grill. Pat snapper dry. Brush with remaining oil. Season with salt. Broil 2 inches from heat source until snapper is just opaque, about 2 minutes per side.

Arrange snapper on platter or plates. Surround with cauliflower. Spoon some of sauce over snapper. Sprinkle with remaining chives. Using slotted spoon, place tomato mixture down both sides of snapper. Pass remaining hollandaise sauce separately.

Baked Fillet of Salmon with Mustard-glazed Cucumbers

An easy-to-prepare entrée. Accompany it with a wild rice pilaf.

6 servings

Vegetable oil
2 1½-pound 1-inch-thick salmon fillets
   Salt and freshly ground pepper
1 cup minced fresh parsley
½ cup minced green onions

3 lemons, thinly sliced
   Mustard-glazed Cucumbers*
2 teaspoons very fine lemon peel julienne
   Fresh tarragon sprigs (optional)

Preheat oven to 450°F. Line baking sheet with foil; grease foil well. Generously oil salmon skin. Place fish skin side down on prepared sheet. Using tweezers, remove any bones. Season with salt and pepper. Combine parsley and green onions and spread over salmon. Cover with lemon slices. Bake until fish is just opaque, about 14 minutes. Remove lemon slices and scrape off loose parsley mixture. Cut each fillet into 3 pieces and transfer to heated platter. Spoon cucumbers down center of each salmon piece. Garnish fish with lemon peel julienne and fresh tarragon.

*Mustard-glazed Cucumbers

6 servings

4 medium cucumbers, peeled, halved lengthwise, seeded and cut into 1½ × ¼-inch strips	1 cup dry white wine
6 tablespoons (¾ stick) unsalted butter	8 teaspoons Dijon mustard
1 cup chopped shallots	2 tablespoons minced fresh tarragon or 2 teaspoons dried, crumbled
	Salt and freshly ground pepper

Cook cucumbers in large pot of boiling water until crisp-tender, 1 to 2 minutes. Drain; rinse with cold water and drain. Pat cucumbers dry. Melt butter in heavy large skillet over medium-high heat. Add shallots and stir 2 minutes. Add wine and mustard and boil until reduced to glaze, about 5 minutes. (*Can be prepared 8 hours ahead. Let stand at room temperature. Reheat glaze before continuing.*) Add cucumber strips and tarragon and stir until cucumbers are heated through. Season with salt and pepper.

Salt Cod and Vegetables in Herbed Tomato Sauce

Start soaking the cod 48 hours before cooking. The recipe easily doubles and is ideal for a buffet. Round out the menu with bread, salad and a medium-bodied red wine.

6 servings

2 pounds dried salt cod, rinsed	3 medium new potatoes, boiled until just tender, peeled and quartered
¼ cup (½ stick) unsalted butter	
3 tablespoons extra-virgin olive oil	
2 medium onions, chopped	1 cup bite-size cauliflower florets, steamed until crisp-tender
4 bay leaves	
2 small fresh thyme sprigs	¼ teaspoon herbes de Provence
1 large garlic clove, minced	18 black Greek olives, pitted
½ teaspoon herbes de Provence*	1 tablespoon (heaping) drained capers
⅛ teaspoon freshly ground pepper	
6 large tomatoes, seeded and chopped	2 ounces feta or mozzarella cheese, thinly sliced

Place cod in large bowl. Cover with cold water. Soak in refrigerator 48 hours, changing water 8 times.

Melt butter with oil in heavy nonaluminum skillet over medium heat. Add onions and cook until golden brown, stirring occasionally, about 12 minutes. Add bay leaves, thyme, garlic, ½ teaspoon herbes de Provence and pepper. Stir until garlic begins to color, about 3 minutes. Add tomatoes. Simmer slowly until sauce mounds in spoon, stirring occasionally, about 40 minutes. Add potatoes and cauliflower. Simmer 15 minutes to blend flavors. (*Can be prepared 4 hours ahead. Let stand at room temperature.*)

Drain cod; rinse well. Cut into 2½-inch pieces. Pat cod dry.

Preheat oven to 350°F. Bring tomato sauce to simmer. Transfer to 12 × 14-inch baking dish. Add cod, turning to coat. Sprinkle with ¼ teaspoon herbes de Provence. Bake 15 minutes. Turn cod to moisten. Sprinkle with olives and capers, then cheese. Bake until cheese melts, about 5 minutes.

*Available at specialty foods stores and some supermarkets.

Sea Bass with Pistou Sauce

The zesty basil sauce is also delicious on halibut, swordfish or salmon.

4 servings

Pistou Sauce
 2 medium garlic cloves
 1 cup lightly packed basil leaves
 1/2 cup olive oil
 1 egg, room temperature
 2 teaspoons fresh lemon juice
 Salt and freshly ground pepper
 1/4 cup vegetable oil

Sea Bass
 1 cup dry white wine
 2 tablespoons olive oil

 1 tablespoon coarsely chopped fresh basil leaves
 Salt and freshly ground pepper
 1 1/2 pounds sea bass fillet (about 1 inch thick), cut into 4 pieces

 12 boiling onions, peeled and cooked until tender
 12 cherry tomatoes
 4 basil sprigs

For sauce: With processor running, drop garlic through feed tube and chop finely. Add basil and 1/4 cup olive oil and coarsely chop basil using on/off turns, stopping to scrape down sides of bowl. Remove basil mixture. Add egg to processor. Blend in 1 tablespoon olive oil, 1 teaspoon lemon juice, salt and pepper. With machine running, add remaining olive oil and vegetable oil through feed tube in thin stream and mix until sauce is thick. Blend in basil-garlic mixture in 2 batches. Add remaining lemon juice. Adjust seasoning. Refrigerate until ready to use. (*Can be prepared 2 days ahead.*)

For bass: Mix wine, olive oil, chopped basil, salt and pepper in shallow bowl. Add bass. Let marinate 1 hour at room temperature, turning twice.

Transfer bass and marinade to large skillet. Bring to simmer, basting bass occasionally. Reduce heat to low, cover and cook until just tender, about 8 minutes. Using slotted spoon, transfer bass to platter or plates. Discard basil adhering to fish. Pour off any exuded liquid. Spoon some of sauce over bass. Surround with onions and tomatoes. Garnish with basil sprigs. Pass remaining sauce separately. Serve bass hot or at room temperature.

Sole with Noodles

4 servings

Sole
 1 to 1 1/2 pounds sole fillets
 Salt and freshly ground pepper
 1 tablespoon chopped shallot
 1 medium tomato, peeled, seeded and coarsely chopped
 1 1/3 cups fish stock or clam juice
 1 cup dry white wine

 1 cup whipping cream

Hollandaise
 1 cup (2 sticks) unsalted butter, cut into small pieces
 3 egg yolks, room temperature
 4 tablespoons fresh lemon juice
 2 teaspoons cold water
 Cayenne pepper

 12 ounces egg noodles or fettuccine

For sole: Preheat oven to 375°F. Generously butter large flameproof baking dish. Arrange sole fillets in single layer, folding slightly to fit if necessary. Season with salt and pepper. Sprinkle with shallot. Scatter tomato over. Add stock and wine. Cover with buttered parchment or waxed paper. Bring liquid just to boil over medium heat. Transfer to oven. Bake until sole is just firm, 2 to 3 minutes.

Pour liquid from dish into heavy medium saucepan. Boil until reduced to ½ cup. Add ½ cup cream and boil until sauce thickens, about 5 minutes.

For hollandaise: Melt butter in heavy small saucepan. Remove from heat. Off heat, whisk yolks, 2 tablespoons lemon juice and water in double boiler until light, about 30 seconds. Set over gently simmering water and whisk until creamy and thick, about 5 minutes. Remove from over water. Whisk in butter in thin stream. Blend in remaining 2 tablespoons lemon juice. Season with salt and cayenne pepper.

Preheat broiler. Cook noodles in large pot of boiling salted water until just tender but firm to bite. Drain, rinse and drain again. Mix noodles with remaining ½ cup cream in shallow gratin dish. Drain any exuded fish juices into cream sauce. Arrange fish over noodles. Whisk hollandaise into cream sauce. Adjust seasoning with salt, pepper, cayenne and lemon juice. Spoon sauce over fish. Broil until golden and bubbly and serve.

Turbot with Lemon and Herbs

This light entrée can also be baked in a gratin pan covered with aluminum foil.

4 servings

½ cup (1 stick) butter
1 cup carrot julienne
1 cup fennel julienne
1 cup leek julienne (white part only)
1 cup celery julienne
1 cup onion julienne
   Salt and freshly ground pepper

4 ¼-pound turbot fillets
4 anchovy fillets, rinsed and drained
4 thin lemon rounds
4 tarragon sprigs
4 thyme sprigs
4 rosemary sprigs
   All purpose flour

Melt butter in heavy skillet over medium heat. Add vegetables and cook until crisp-tender, stirring occasionally, 7 to 10 minutes. Season with salt and pepper.

Preheat oven to 375°F. Make incision down center of each turbot fillet; do not cut through. Place anchovy fillet in each. Divide vegetables among 4 individual terrine molds with lids. Set turbot fillet in each. Top each with lemon round, then 1 sprig of each herb. Sprinkle with salt and pepper. Cover molds. Make paste of flour and water. Spread over seam between lid and dish of molds to seal tightly. Bake 15 minutes. Serve immediately.

Trout Forestière

6 servings

6 tablespoons (¾ stick) unsalted butter, clarified
6 8-ounce trout fillets, heads removed, tails left intact
   All purpose flour
2 eggs beaten with 1 tablespoon water
2 cups dry breadcrumbs

2 cups thinly sliced mushrooms
¾ cup dry white wine

¾ cup sliced green onions
¼ cup whipping cream
3 tablespoons fresh lemon juice
2 teaspoons minced garlic
   Seafood Seasoning*
6 tablespoons (¾ stick) well-chilled unsalted butter, cut into pieces

Heat clarified butter in heavy large skillet over medium heat. Dredge fish in flour, shaking off excess. Dip fish in egg mixture and then in breadcrumbs, coating completely. Add fish to skillet (in batches, if necessary) and cook until golden brown and just opaque, about 3 minutes per side. Transfer to platter. Tent with foil to keep fish warm.

Increase heat to medium-high. Add mushrooms to skillet and stir until just tender, about 3 minutes. Add wine, onions, cream, lemon juice, garlic and Seafood Seasoning and cook until liquid is reduced by half, stirring occasionally. Whisk in 6 tablespoons butter 1 piece at a time. Spoon mushroom sauce over trout. Serve immediately.

*Seafood Seasoning

Makes about 2 tablespoons

2½ teaspoons salt
  1 teaspoon freshly ground pepper
  1 teaspoon granulated garlic
  ¾ teaspoon paprika

¾ teaspoon granulated onion
¼ teaspoon cayenne pepper
⅛ teaspoon dried thyme, crumbled

Combine all ingredients in small bowl. Store seasoning at room temperature in container with tight-fitting lid.

Steamed Fish with Hard Cider, Apples and Celery Root

A delicate main course. Rub the celery root and apples with lemon as soon as they are peeled to prevent their becoming discolored.

4 servings

2¼ pounds firm white-fleshed fish such as turbot or whitefish, filleted (bones reserved)
  6 cups hard cider
  1 cup dry white wine
  1 medium onion, halved
    Bouquet garni (3 parsley sprigs, 1 bay leaf, 1 thyme sprig)

3½ ounces shallots, minced
  4 tablespoons hard cider
    Salt and freshly ground pepper

¼ cup (½ stick) butter
  1 pound celery root, peeled and thinly sliced
  1 pound tart green apples, peeled, cored and thinly sliced

¼ cup crème fraîche
½ cup (1 stick) butter, cut into 8 pieces

Rinse fish bones. Combine bones, 6 cups cider, wine, onion and bouquet garni in large pot. Simmer 25 minutes. Strain fumet into medium saucepan. Boil until reduced to scant 1 cup.

Butter four 8-inch squares of foil. Sprinkle with shallots. Divide fish among foil squares. Sprinkle each with 1 tablespoon cider. Season with salt and pepper. Fold foil over fish and seal.

Melt ¼ cup butter in heavy large skillet over medium heat. Add celery root and cook until almost tender, stirring frequently, about 10 minutes. Add apples and stir until apples and celery root are tender, about 5 minutes.

Meanwhile, bring water to boil in base of steamer. Place packages of fish on steamer rack. Cover and cook until fish is just opaque, about 9 minutes per inch of thickness. Remove packages from steamer; open foil and add cooking liquid in packages to fumet. Reseal foil. Bring fumet to simmer. Add crème fraîche and simmer until reduced by ⅓. Remove from heat and whisk in butter 1 piece at a time. Season sauce with salt and pepper. Divide among 4 heated plates. Remove fish from foil and place on sauce. Arrange apple and celery root around fish. Serve immediately.

Steamed Seafood with Basil and Mint Pistou

On a warm summer night this would be an ideal party dish. Uncork a Muscadet or other dry white wine.

6 to 8 servings

3 large garlic cloves
¹/₈ teaspoon salt
2¹/₂ cups lightly packed fresh basil
¹/₄ cup lightly packed fresh mint
¹/₂ cup extra-virgin olive oil
¹/₄ cup freshly grated Parmesan cheese (preferably imported)
¹/₄ cup shredded Gruyère cheese

2¹/₂ cups chicken stock
3 medium shallots, chopped
2 whole cloves
1 4-inch strip orange peel (orange part only)

1 pound bluefish, bass or halibut fillets
1 pound cod fillets
Salt and freshly ground pepper
1 pound large shrimp, peeled (tail sections left on) and deveined
2 pounds littleneck or cherrystone clams, scrubbed
1 pound mussels, scrubbed and debearded

4 large tomatoes, seeded and diced
Fresh basil sprigs

Mash garlic and salt to paste in mortar with pestle. Coarsely chop 2¹/₂ cups basil and mint in processor. Add garlic paste. With machine running, slowly pour oil in through feed tube. Mix in cheeses using on/off turns. (*Can be prepared 8 hours ahead. Cover tightly and store at room temperature.*)

Preheat oven to 200°F. Bring stock, shallots, cloves and orange peel to gentle simmer in base of steamer. Grease steamer rack and place over simmering liquid. Sprinkle fish fillets lightly with salt and pepper. Arrange on rack. Cover and steam until just opaque, about 9 minutes per inch of thickness. Transfer to platter, using spatula. Tent with foil and keep warm in oven. Place shrimp on steamer rack. Cover and cook until just firm, 3 to 4 minutes. Transfer to platter with fish. Remove steamer rack. Add clams and mussels to steaming liquid. Cover and simmer gently until shells open, 5 to 10 minutes. Transfer to platter with fish, using slotted spoon and discarding any shells that do not open.

Return pistou to processor. Add ¹/₄ cup steaming liquid and blend. Drizzle some of pistou over fish. Scatter tomatoes over. Garnish with basil sprigs. Serve seafood immediately, passing remaining pistou separately.

Seafood Gratin

Ginger and saffron add a special nuance to this crumb-topped mélange.

4 to 6 servings

¹/₂ cup dry white wine
6 shallots, coarsely chopped
Bouquet garni (parsley, bay leaf, thyme)
1 quart mussels, scrubbed and debearded

1 pound halibut fillets, skinned, boned and cut into 1-inch cubes
1 pound salmon fillets, skinned, boned and cut into 1-inch cubes
1 teaspoon ground ginger

Saffron Ginger Sauce
2 cups Fish Fumet*
1 cup whipping cream
3 tablespoons butter

1 onion, chopped
¹/₂ carrot, chopped
Bouquet garni (parsley, bay leaf, thyme)
3 tablespoons all purpose flour
Salt and freshly ground pepper
¹/₄ cup grated fresh ginger
¹/₈ teaspoon ground saffron

¹/₄ cup chopped fresh parsley
1 cup fresh breadcrumbs
¹/₄ cup (¹/₂ stick) butter, melted

Combine wine, shallots and bouquet garni in large pot. Add mussels. Cover and steam over high heat 5 minutes, shaking pan occasionally. Remove opened mussels. Cook remaining mussels 5 minutes more; discard any that do not open. Strain mussel cooking liquid through strainer lined with several layers of dampened cheesecloth and reserve. Shell mussels.

Combine halibut and salmon in medium bowl. Mix in ground ginger. Cover while preparing sauce.

For sauce: Combine fumet, cream and 1 cup mussel cooking liquid in heavy small saucepan. Heat until very hot. Remove from heat. Melt 3 tablespoons butter in heavy large saucepan over medium-low heat. Add onion, carrot and bouquet garni. Cook until onion is translucent, stirring occasionally, about 8 minutes. Add flour and cook until straw colored, stirring frequently, about 5 minutes. Remove from heat. Gradually whisk in heated liquids. Bring to boil over medium-high heat, whisking constantly. Reduce heat to low and cook until reduced to 2½ cups, skimming occasionally, about 10 minutes. Season with salt and pepper. Strain sauce through fine sieve into another large saucepan. Mix in ginger and saffron.

Preheat broiler. Butter 13 × 9-inch gratin dish. Bring sauce to boil. Add halibut and salmon and stir until fish is just opaque, about 3 minutes. Remove from heat. Add mussels and parsley. Adjust seasoning. Spoon mixture into prepared dish. Mix breadcrumbs with ¼ cup melted butter. Sprinkle over fish. Broil until topping is golden brown, about 5 minutes.

---

*Fish Fumet

Makes about 4 cups

4 pounds heads and bones from nonoily white fish, rinsed	2 carrots, sliced
	6 parsley stems
4 cups water	12 whole black peppercorns
1 cup dry white wine	1 bay leaf
2 onions, sliced	1 teaspoon fresh lemon juice
2 celery stalks, sliced	

Combine all ingredients in large saucepan. Bring to boil, skimming surface. Reduce heat and simmer 30 minutes. Strain through fine sieve. (*Can be prepared ahead and refrigerated 2 days or frozen up to 3 months.*)

7 ❦ Vegetables, Grains and Breads

Whether they come from the family garden or a vendor at the Saturday open-air market, fresh vegetables are an essential part of the French meal. From the first tender peas and *haricots verts* of spring to the last cabbages of fall, to the squashes and hearty root vegetables of winter, vegetables are cooked in a dazzling number of ways. Among our offerings: easy Warm Green Beans in Walnut Oil (page 82), colorful Carrot, Pea and Salsify Sauté (page 83), traditional Potato Galette (page 83), Spring Vegetable Ragout (page 84) and basic Vegetable Gratins (page 84) with a variety of sauces.

Although potato is a favorite starch, rice is often served with meat and poultry. We offer two recipes: a Mediterranean Rice Pilaf (page 86) and Wild Rice Pilaf with Carrots and Fennel (page 87).

It has been said that France is a country of bread-lovers, and some would even argue that the national emblem should not be the fleur-de-lis but the ubiquitous *baguette*. Bread is served at every meal, and many dishes, from soups to pâtés, are made to be eaten with bread. While most people buy their daily bread from the local *boulanger*, we offer a few basics that can be prepared easily at home, including the flat country *fougasse* or Hearth Bread (page 87), Country-style Rye Rolls (page 90) and Gruyère Baguettes (page 89). There's even a Rich Brioche with Caramelized Almond Topping (page 91) and a robust Chestnut and Dried Pear Bread (page 94) to munch for dessert.

 *Vegetables*

Warm Green Beans in Walnut Oil

6 servings

1 pound green beans, trimmed

1 tablespoon red wine vinegar
2 garlic cloves, minced

Salt and freshly ground pepper
3 tablespoons walnut oil

Blanch beans in boiling salted water until crisp-tender, about 5 minutes. Drain.
Blend vinegar, garlic, salt and pepper in large bowl. Whisk in oil in thin stream. Mix in beans. Let stand several minutes. Toss and serve.

White Beans with Tomatoes and Herbs

8 servings

1 pound dried navy beans, sorted

1 medium onion, quartered
1 tablespoon salt

1½ cups parsley leaves
2 large garlic cloves
1 small onion, quartered

2 tablespoons olive oil
Marinade reserved from Marinated Lamb Roast* (see page 53)

¾ to 1 cup beef broth
½ cup tomato paste
1 tablespoon Sherry wine vinegar
1½ teaspoons dried basil, crumbled
1¼ teaspoons salt
½ teaspoon ground cumin
Freshly ground pepper

2 large tomatoes, cored and halved vertically

Soak dried navy beans in enough cold water to cover overnight.
Drain beans. Transfer to 6-quart saucepan. Add medium onion, 1 tablespoon salt and enough cold water to cover. Bring to boil. Reduce heat, cover and simmer until beans are just tender, 45 minutes. Drain well, discarding onion.
Finely mince parsley in processor. Set aside. With machine running, drop garlic and small onion through feed tube and mince finely. Heat oil in heavy 10-inch skillet over low heat. Add garlic and onion and cook until soft, stirring frequently, about 12 minutes. Add marinade, ¾ cup broth, tomato paste, vinegar, basil, 1¼ teaspoons salt, cumin and pepper. Bring to boil. Reduce heat and simmer 5 minutes, stirring frequently. Add beans and cook 10 minutes. (*Can be prepared 1 day ahead. Cool and refrigerate. Reheat mixture before continuing, adding more beef broth if necessary.*)
Insert french fry disc in processor. Arrange 1 tomato half in feed tube cut side down. Cut using light pressure. Transfer to beans, using slotted spoon. Repeat with remaining halves. Stir over low heat until warmed through. Add reserved parsley to beans and serve immediately.

*If marinade is not available, substitute ½ cup dry red wine, ¼ cup Sherry wine vinegar, ¼ cup olive oil, 1 teaspoon dried oregano, crumbled, and ½ teaspoon salt.

❧

Potato Galette

For the best presentation, select potatoes that are uniform in size, or trim them to the same shape.

6 servings

¾ cup (1½ sticks) unsalted butter

3 long, thin, 8-ounce baking potatoes, peeled

½ teaspoon salt
Freshly ground pepper

Position rack in center of oven and preheat to 400°F. Melt butter in heavy small saucepan over low heat. Skim foam from surface. Let stand 10 minutes. Carefully pour clear butter into heavy 10-inch ovenproof skillet, discarding butter sediment in saucepan.

Stand one potato in processor feed tube and thinly slice, using firm pressure. Heat butter over medium heat. Arrange potato slices in skillet, starting from center of pan and overlapping in concentric circles toward edge. Season with some of salt and pepper. Repeat with remaining potatoes, slicing 1 at a time and leaving pan on heat.

Increase heat to medium-high. Cook galette until edges and bottom are brown, about 8 minutes. Place in oven and bake 10 minutes. Carefully turn galette, using spatula. Return skillet to stove top and cook over medium-high heat 3 minutes. Return to oven and bake until bottom is well browned and potatoes are tender, about 10 minutes. Drain galette on paper towels. Blot excess butter on top. Serve immediately.

Rutabaga Puree

Makes about 2½ cups

2 medium rutabagas, peeled and cubed
1 chicken bouillon cube
Salt and freshly ground pepper

6 tablespoons (¾ stick) butter
2 tablespoons minced fresh parsley
1 small garlic clove, minced

Cover rutabagas with cold water in large saucepan and bring to boil. Add bouillon cube and salt and pepper. Reduce heat and simmer until rutabagas are very tender, about 15 minutes.

Drain rutabagas. Transfer to processor. Add butter and blend until fluffy. Adjust seasoning. Add parsley and garlic and mix 30 seconds. Turn into bowl and serve immediately.

Carrot, Pea and Salsify Sauté

4 servings

3 ounces side pork*
1 tablespoon bacon fat, goose fat or butter
1 pound carrots, peeled and cut into ½-inch rounds

1 pound fresh or frozen peas
½ pound salsify,** peeled, blanched 5 minutes and cut into 2-inch pieces
Salt and freshly ground pepper

Remove skin from side pork, leaving as much fat as possible. Cut side pork into ¼-inch-thick slices. Cut slices crosswise into ¼-inch strips.

Melt fat in heavy large skillet over medium-high heat. Add side pork and sauté until golden brown, about 5 minutes. Reduce heat to medium. Add carrots and fresh peas and sauté 2 minutes. Cover and cook until carrots are softened but not cooked through about 8 minutes. Increase heat to medium-high. Add frozen peas and sauté 3 minutes. Add salsify and sauté until tender, about 3 minutes. Season with salt and pepper. Serve immediately.

*If unavailable, salt pork can be substituted. Blanch 5 minutes before using.
**If fresh is unavailable, use canned.

Spring Vegetable Ragout

6 to 8 servings

1 pound fresh peas, shelled, 10 pods reserved and thinly sliced
3 fresh watercress sprigs
20 white pearl onions, peeled
6 tablespoons (³/₄ stick) butter

¹/₂ cup morel liquid or strained mushroom soaking liquid (see page 50)
1 teaspoon sugar
Salt and freshly ground pepper

Boil peas, pods and watercress in several quarts of boiling salted water 3 minutes. Drain, rinse under cold water and drain again. Transfer to heavy skillet. Add onions, butter, ¹/₄ cup morel liquid, sugar, salt and pepper. Cover tightly and braise over medium-low heat until vegetables are tender, about 30 minutes, adding remaining morel liquid if mixture seems too dry. Adjust seasoning.

Vegetable Gratin

For vegetable suggestions and additional tips, see Variations.

4 servings

1¹/₂ pounds fresh vegetables
Salt
1¹/₃ cups hot Cream Sauce,* Cheese Sauce* or Fresh Tomato Sauce**

2 tablespoons freshly grated Parmesan cheese, breadcrumbs or chopped nuts

Preheat oven to 425°F. Butter heavy 5-cup gratin dish or shallow baking dish. Prepare vegetables (see below). Cook vegetables in large pot of boiling salted water until just tender when pierced with sharp knife. Drain vegetables. Rinse under cold water until cool; drain thoroughly. Arrange in prepared dish. Carefully spoon sauce over vegetables to coat completely. (*Can be prepared 1 day ahead, covered and refrigerated. Bring to room temperature before baking.*) Sprinkle evenly with cheese, crumbs or nuts. Bake until sauce bubbles, 7 to 10 minutes. If top is not browned, broil with oven door partially open about 1 minute, watching carefully to prevent burning. Serve hot.

For broccoli gratin: Cut broccoli into medium florets. Discard leaves; reserve large stalks for another use.

For cabbage gratin: Cut out and discard core. Shred cabbage coarsely. After cooking and draining, squeeze cabbage to remove excess water.

For cauliflower gratin: Cut cauliflower into florets; discard stalks and leaves.

For leek gratin: Use white and light green parts only. Halve lengthwise, then cut into 1-inch pieces. Rinse well. Continue cooking until tender. After cooking and draining, pat dry.

For Swiss chard gratin: Cut leaves from ribs; reserve ribs for another use. Rinse leaves thoroughly. Stack leaves, halve lengthwise, then cut crosswise into ¹/₂-inch strips. After cooking and draining, squeeze to remove excess water.

For winter squash gratin: Use banana or hubbard squash. Remove seeds and strings with spoon. Cut squash into 2 × 2 × 1-inch pieces. After cooking and draining, peel, then drain thoroughly.

*Cream Sauce

Makes about 1¹/₃ cups

2 **tablespoons (¹/₄ stick) unsalted butter**	**Salt and freshly ground pepper**
2 **tablespoons all purpose flour**	**Freshly grated nutmeg**
1¹/₂ **cups milk**	¹/₄ **cup whipping cream**
	Cayenne pepper

Melt 2 tablespoons butter in heavy medium saucepan over low heat. Add flour and whisk until foaming but not browned, about 3 minutes. Remove from heat. Gradually whisk in milk. Bring to boil over medium-high heat, whisking constantly. Add salt, pepper and nutmeg. Reduce heat to low and cook 5 minutes, whisking frequently. Whisk in cream; return to boil. Reduce heat to low and cook until sauce thickens and coats back of spoon, whisking frequently, about 7 minutes. Remove from heat. Stir in cayenne. Adjust seasoning. (*Sauce can be prepared 1 day ahead. Dot surface with additional butter. Cover with plastic wrap and refrigerate. Reheat before using.*)

For cheese sauce: Whisk ¹/₄ cup freshly grated Parmesan cheese into sauce.

**Fresh Tomato Sauce

Makes 1¹/₃ cups

2 **tablespoons olive oil**	1 **bay leaf**
2 **garlic cloves, minced**	**Salt and freshly ground pepper**
2 **pounds ripe tomatoes, peeled, seeded and chopped**	1 **tablespoon tomato paste**
1 **teaspoon chopped fresh thyme or ¹/₄ teaspoon dried, crumbled**	**Pinch of sugar (optional)**

Heat oil in heavy large saucepan over low heat. Add garlic and stir until soft but not browned, about 30 seconds. Stir in tomatoes, thyme, bay leaf, salt and pepper. Bring to boil. Reduce heat to low and cook until tomatoes are very soft and sauce is thick, stirring occasionally, about 1 hour.

Discard bay leaf. Puree sauce in processor or blender until smooth. Return to saucepan and whisk in tomato paste. Bring to boil. Reduce heat to low and cook until sauce is very thick and reduced to 1¹/₃ cups, stirring occasionally, about 10 minutes. Add sugar if desired. Adjust seasoning. (*Sauce can be prepared 1 day ahead, covered and refrigerated. Reheat before using.*)

Variations

Gratins are very versatile: All three essential elements—the vegetables, sauce and topping—can be easily modified to create new versions. The proportions and principles outlined in the Vegetable Gratin recipe can be applied to many different vegetables. Practice mixing and matching with the suggestions here. A little more of one ingredient and a little less of another will not significantly change the result. Use the vegetables you have on hand.

Leek and mushroom gratin: Finely chop mushrooms and shallots. Sauté in butter. Spoon mushroom mixture into gratin dish. Top with cooked leeks. Coat with Cream Sauce. Sprinkle with grated Gruyère cheese.

Gratin of Swiss chard with bell peppers: Seed green pepper and cut into thin strips. Sauté in olive oil. Layer in gratin dish with cooked Swiss chard and Fresh Tomato Sauce. Sprinkle gratin with breadcrumbs and chopped almonds. Drizzle with olive oil.

Belgian endive, ham and cheese gratin: Halve cooked endive lengthwise. Arrange in gratin dish. Top with thin ham slices. Coat with Cheese Sauce. Sprinkle with Parmesan cheese.

Zucchini and pearl onion gratin: Halve small zucchini lengthwise, then cut crosswise into 2-inch pieces. Cook until just tender. Drain thoroughly. Layer in gratin dish with cooked pearl onions. Coat with Fresh Tomato Sauce. Sprinkle with grated Parmesan cheese or chopped nuts.

Artichoke and cauliflower gratin: Arrange chopped cooked artichoke hearts in gratin dish. Top with chopped cooked cauliflower. Coat with Cheese Sauce. Sprinkle sauce with freshly grated Parmesan cheese.

Crunchy broccoli gratin: Arrange cooked broccoli in gratin dish. Drizzle with melted butter. Sprinkle with mixture of grated sharp cheddar cheese, chopped pecans and breadcrumbs.

Easy eggplant gratin: Sauté eggplant slices in olive oil (do not precook). Layer in gratin dish with sautéed white or green onions. Sprinkle with grated Gruyère or provolone cheese.

 Grains

Mediterranean Rice Pilaf

4 to 6 servings

1 lemon, halved
4 medium artichokes

4 cups salted water
1 tablespoon fresh lemon juice

Saffron Water
2 cups salted water
1/4 teaspoon crushed saffron threads

3 tablespoons olive oil
1 cup minced onion
1 cup long-grain white rice

5 parsley stems
1 fresh thyme sprig or 1/4 teaspoon dried, crumbled
1 bay leaf
1/2 teaspoon salt
Freshly ground pepper
2 medium tomatoes, peeled, seeded, diced and drained

2 tablespoons olive oil
1 zucchini, cut into 1/4-inch cubes
Salt and freshly ground pepper
1 1/2 teaspoons minced fresh cilantro
1/3 cup slivered almonds, toasted

Fill large bowl with water. Add juice of lemon half. Break off stem of artichoke and rub exposed area with remaining lemon half. Starting from base, bend each leaf back and snap off at natural break. Cut off tight cone of leaves above heart. Trim and shape heart carefully with knife until no dark green area remains. Rub with lemon. Place in bowl of water. Repeat with remaining artichokes.

Bring 4 cups salted water to boil in medium saucepan. Drain artichoke hearts. Add 1 tablespoon lemon juice and artichokes to saucepan. Reduce heat to low, cover and cook until tender when pierced with knife, about 15 minutes. Cool artichokes to lukewarm in water. Drain. Scoop out chokes with spoon and discard. Cut artichokes into 1/2-inch pieces.

For saffron water: Bring 2 cups salted water to boil. Add saffron.

Position rack in lower third of oven. Preheat oven to 350°F. Cut parchment paper into 8- to 9 1/2-inch circle; butter paper. Warm 3 tablespoons oil in 8- to 9 1/2-inch ovenproof deep skillet over low heat. Add onion and cook until soft but not brown, stirring occasionally, about 7 minutes. Increase heat to medium. Add rice and sauté until grains turn opaque and milky white, about 4 minutes.

Bring saffron water to boil. Pour over rice, stirring once. Tie parsley, thyme and bay leaf in cheesecloth. Add to rice with salt and pepper. Press parchment buttered side down onto rice. Cover and transfer to oven. Bake until rice is slightly chewy and fluffy and liquid is absorbed, 18 to 20 minutes; do not stir. Spoon tomatoes and artichokes over. Cover and let stand 4 minutes.

Meanwhile, heat 2 tablespoons olive oil in heavy medium skillet over medium heat. Add zucchini, salt and pepper and sauté until just tender, about 1½ minutes. Sprinkle cilantro over rice. Gently stir in zucchini with oil, fluffing rice gently with fork. Top with half of almonds. Serve hot, passing remaining almonds separately.

Wild Rice Pilaf with Carrots and Fennel

Mound on a platter and surround with baked pork chops and mushrooms for a pretty presentation.

6 servings

2 quarts water
1½ cups wild rice

2 medium fennel bulbs, tough outer layer discarded, trimmed, halved and cored
10 tablespoons (1¼ sticks) unsalted butter
4 medium carrots, peeled and cut into 1½ × ¼-inch julienne

1 cup chopped onion
1 cup converted rice
1 teaspoon dried ground thyme
1 teaspoon dried tarragon, crumbled
1 teaspoon salt
4 cups beef stock
1 cup dry white wine
  Minced fresh parsley

Bring water to boil in heavy large saucepan. Add wild rice and boil 10 minutes. Drain well.

Cut fennel lengthwise into ¼-inch-thick slices. Melt butter in heavy Dutch oven over medium heat. Add fennel and carrots and stir 4 minutes. Add onion and stir 3 minutes. Add wild and converted rice. Stir to coat with butter. Mix in thyme, tarragon and salt. Add stock and wine. Bring to boil. Reduce heat to low, cover and cook until rice is just tender and all liquid is absorbed, stirring occasionally, 40 minutes. Top with parsley.

 Breads

Hearth Bread

A specialty of southern France, this flat bread resembles Italy's focaccia.

Makes 2 loaves

1 tablespoon dry yeast
3 cups warm water (105° to 115°F)
4 cups (or more) unbleached all purpose flour

1 tablespoon salt dissolved in 1 tablespoon warm water
2 cups whole wheat flour

Sprinkle yeast over warm water in large bowl and let stand until dissolved; stir to blend. Stir in 4 cups all purpose flour 1 cup at a time. Using wooden spoon or hands, beat mixture vigorously 3 minutes. Blend in dissolved salt. Gradually beat in as much whole wheat flour as dough will absorb. Turn dough out onto generously floured surface and knead in remaining whole wheat flour. Continue kneading until dough is firm and smooth yet slightly sticky, adding more all purpose flour if necessary, about 5 minutes. Form dough into ball. Dust with all purpose flour. Cover with towel. Let dough rise in warm draft-free area until doubled in volume, about 2 hours.

Flour baking sheets. Punch dough down. Divide in half. Roll out each piece into 9 × 12-inch oblong with thickness of ½ inch. Fold each oblong in half and transfer to prepared sheet. Unfold dough. Run rolling pin over top to smooth. Using sharp knife, cut slits through dough in spoke pattern, radiating from center. Pull slits apart to form holes. Cover dough with towel. Let rise in warm draft-free area until about 1 inch high, about 1 hour.

Preheat oven to 375°F. Bake until bread is crisp and golden brown, 40 to 45 minutes. Serve warm.

Pain Ordinaire

This versatile dough can be formed into several shapes. There are also two flavor variations: For whole wheat French bread, substitute 1½ cups finely ground whole wheat flour for the same amount of unbleached all purpose flour. Or create loaves similar to San Francisco sourdough by using 2 cups warm yogurt instead of warm water.

Makes 4 baguettes

1½ **packages dry yeast or 1½ cakes fresh yeast**
1 **teaspoon sugar**
2 **cups warm or lukewarm water (see below)**

2¾ **cups bread flour**
2¾ **cups unbleached all purpose flour**
2 **teaspoons salt**

Additional unbleached all purpose flour

Cornmeal

1 **egg white blended with 1 tablespoon water and pinch of salt (glaze)**

Sprinkle dry yeast and sugar over warm water (105°F to 115°F) in large bowl of heavy-duty electric mixer; stir to dissolve. If using cake yeast, crumble into bowl. Stir in sugar and lukewarm water (95°F). Let stand until foamy, about 10 minutes.

Combine bread flour and 2¾ cups all purpose flour in another bowl. Add 2 cups flour mixture and salt to yeast. Using wire whisk attachment of electric mixer, beat 5 minutes to develop gluten (dough can also be made by hand using balloon whisk). Remove wire whisk from mixer and insert paddle. Using low speed, blend in enough remaining flour mixture ½ cup at a time to form dough that cleans sides of bowl. Knead on floured surface until smooth and elastic, kneading in additional all purpose flour if sticky (pick dough up occasionally and slap onto surface to develop gluten), about 12 minutes.

Grease large bowl. Add dough, turning to coat entire surface. Cover bowl with plastic. Let dough rise in cool area until tripled in volume, about 2 hours. (*Dough can also be refrigerated for slow rise.*)

Gently knead dough in bowl to deflate. Cover and let rise in cool place again until tripled in volume, about 1½ hours. (*Dough can also be covered and refrigerated for slow rise.*)

Sprinkle cornmeal on ungreased baking sheets or French bread pans. Gently knead dough on lightly floured surface until deflated, kneading in additional all purpose flour if sticky. Cut into 4 even pieces. Flatten each into rectangle. Roll up jelly roll fashion, starting at 1 long end. Pinch seams to seal. Roll back and forth on work surface until dough is length of pan. Arrange seam side down on prepared sheets, spacing at least 4 inches apart. Let rise 25 minutes to lighten.

Position rack in lower third of oven. Set baking stones on rack if desired. Preheat oven to 425°F. Slash top of loaves, using serrated knife. Brush with glaze. Bake until loaves sound hollow when tapped on bottom, about 25 minutes. Immediately transfer to racks. Serve hot, warm or at room temperature. Can be reheated in 400°F oven for about 5 minutes.

Clockwise from top right: Coupes Plougastel; Shortbread Brittany Style; Little Prune Turnovers; Applejack Cake Filled with Candied Apples; Cream Cheese with Pear and Cider Butter

Jerry Friedman

Irwin Horowitz

Counterclockwise from right: Beet Salad with Marinated Turnip Slices; Hearth Bread; Fresh Tomato Sauce; Eggplant and Parmesan Soufflé; Fresh Peach Tart

Clockwise from top right: Pork Chops Baked with Chestnuts, Mushrooms and Onions on Wild Rice Pilaf with Carrots and Fennel; Cream of Butternut Squash and Leek Soup; Wine- and Ginger-marinated Fruit; Spiced Madeleines

Jerry Friedman

Clockwise from top: Sugar Tart with Plum Compote; Grilled Ham Steaks with Onions and Raisins; Escarole Salad with Bacon, Vegetables and Fried Onions; Game and Pistachio Sausages; Lobster, Oyster and Zucchini Tartlets in Champagne Sauce

Clockwise from bottom left: Apple Sauce Fritters; Caramelized Fig Tart; Pear Cake; Savoie-style Chocolate Truffles

Irwin Horowitz

Variations

For 2 batards (*thick ovals*): Cut dough into 2 even pieces. Flatten each into rectangle. Roll up jelly roll fashion, starting at 1 long end. Pinch seams to seal. Taper ends, forming thick oval shapes. Let rise as for baguettes. Bake batards for about 35 to 40 minutes.

For 6 ficelles (*small baguettes*): Cut dough into 6 pieces. Form; let rise as for baguettes. Bake about 20 minutes.

For 1 pain de campagne (*country loaf*): Knead dough into 1 round. Let rise as for baguettes. Bake 45 to 50 minutes.

For 6 champignons (*small "mushroom" shapes*): Cut dough into 6 even pieces. Cut ⅔ off 1 piece of dough and knead into round. Place on prepared sheet. Make well in center. Knead remaining dough piece into round and set in well atop first piece. With floured finger, make hole down center of rounds to baking sheet. Repeat with remaining pieces of dough. Let rise as for baguettes. Bake 20 to 25 minutes.

For 4 boules (*rounds*): Cut dough into 4 even pieces. Knead each into round. Let rise as for baguettes. Slash top. Bake 25 to 30 minutes.

For 4 l'épis (*"sprig" shapes*): Cut dough into 4 even pieces. Form each into 12-inch baguette. Using scissors, cut ¾ of way into dough at 3-inch intervals. Pull each section out in opposite directions and twist slightly to form loaves resembling wheat sprigs. Let rise as for baguettes. Bake for 25 to 30 minutes.

Gruyère Baguettes

Makes 2 loaves

2 tablespoons firmly packed light brown sugar
1 envelope dry yeast
1 cup warm water (105°F to 115°F)

1½ ounces Gruyère cheese (preferably imported), cut into 1-inch pieces
2¼ cups bread flour (or more)
¾ cup rye flour

2 tablespoons (¼ stick) unsalted butter, room temperature
1½ teaspoons salt

Cornmeal

1 egg beaten with ½ teaspoon salt (glaze)

Sprinkle sugar and yeast over water in small bowl; stir to dissolve. Let stand until foamy, about 10 minutes.

Finely mince cheese in processor. Set aside. Combine 2¼ cups bread flour, rye flour, butter and salt in work bowl. With machine running, pour yeast mixture through feed tube and process until dough cleans sides of work bowl. If dough sticks to bowl, add bread flour 1 tablespoon at a time through feed tube, incorporating each addition before adding next. If dough is dry and hard, add water 1 teaspoon at a time through feed tube, incorporating each addition before adding next. Process dough until elastic, about 40 seconds.

Oil large bowl. Add dough, turning to coat entire surface. Cover with oiled plastic wrap. Let dough rise in warm draft-free area until doubled in volume, about 1¼ hours.

Grease double French loaf pan or baking sheet and sprinkle with cornmeal. Punch dough down and divide into 2 pieces. Roll each piece out on lightly floured surface to 10 × 12-inch rectangle. Starting at 1 long end, roll dough up as for jelly roll. Pinch seams to seal. Place loaves seam side down in prepared pan or on baking sheet. Cover with oiled plastic wrap and let rise in warm draft-free area until doubled in volume, about 1¼ hours.

Position rack in center of oven and preheat to 425°F. Brush loaves with glaze. Cut 3 long diagonal slashes ¾ inch deep in top of each loaf, using sharp knife. Spoon 2 teaspoons minced cheese into each slash. Bake bread until light brown and loaves sound hollow when tapped on bottom, about 20 minutes. Transfer to racks. Cool before serving.

Pepper Seed Thin Breads

These spicy crackerlike breads are delightful with fruit, cheese or salad. They are best served the same day they are made.

Makes 10 breads

½ teaspoon fennel seed
½ teaspoon aniseed
2¼ cups all purpose flour
1 tablespoon sugar
1 teaspoon salt
1 teaspoon baking powder
½ teaspoon coarsely ground pepper
½ cup water
¼ cup vegetable oil

Bruise fennel and aniseed in mortar with pestle or with rolling pin. Mix with flour, sugar, salt, baking powder and pepper in large bowl. Make well in center of dry ingredients. Add water and oil to well. Gradually draw flour from inner edge of well into center until all flour is incorporated. Knead dough on lightly floured surface until smooth ball forms. Cover with plastic. Let dough rest 15 minutes. (*Can be prepared 1 day ahead and refrigerated.*)

Position rack in center of oven and preheat to 450°F. Grease baking sheet. Divide dough into 10 pieces. Roll 2 pieces into 8-inch rounds (cover remaining dough). Arrange on prepared sheet. Bake until light brown, about 8 minutes. Cool on rack. Continue rolling and baking remaining dough.

Country-style Rye Rolls

Makes 8

1 tablespoon dry yeast
2 cups warm water (105°F to 115°F)

2¾ cups all purpose flour

1½ cups rye flour

1 tablespoon salt

Sprinkle yeast over water in large bowl and let stand until dissolved; stir to blend. Let stand 10 minutes.

Add 1 cup all purpose flour and 1 cup rye flour and beat dough vigorously 3 minutes. Cover and let rise in warm draft-free area until more than doubled in volume, about 1 hour.

Gradually add remaining flours and salt to dough, stirring well after each addition. Knead dough 5 minutes; dough will be sticky. Cover and let rise in warm draft-free area until more than doubled, about 1½ hours.

Generously flour baking sheet. Divide dough into 8 pieces. Shape each piece into round. Arrange rounds on prepared sheet. Cover and let rise in warm draft-free area until more than doubled in volume, about 1½ hours.

Preheat oven to 375°F. Using sharp knife, cut X atop each roll. Bake until golden brown, 20 to 25 minutes. Cool.

Onion Rolls

These rolls make exceptional sandwich buns.

Makes 15 rolls

½ cup (1 stick) unsalted butter
2 large onions, coarsely chopped
¼ cup whipping cream

1 recipe Pain Ordinaire dough (see page 88)

Cornmeal
Unbleached all purpose flour

Melt butter in heavy large skillet over low heat. Add onions and cook until soft, stirring frequently, about 10 minutes. Add cream, increase heat and boil until liquid evaporates, about 5 minutes. Cool to room temperature.

After second rising of Pain Ordinaire dough, preheat oven to 425°F. Sprinkle baking sheets generously with cornmeal. Gently knead dough on lightly floured surface until deflated, kneading in all purpose flour if sticky.

Cut evenly into 15 pieces. Knead each into round. Arrange on prepared sheets, spacing 3 inches apart. Using scissors, cut ½-inch-deep X in top of each. Pull dough open and make depression in center ¾ of the way to bottom. Fill each with 2 tablespoons onion. Bake until golden brown and rolls sound hollow when tapped on bottom, about 20 minutes. Serve immediately.

Rich Brioche with Caramelized Almond Topping

The special loaf pan used here is available in cookware stores.

8 to 10 servings

Brioche with Almond Filling
1 envelope plus 1 teaspoon dry yeast
¼ cup sugar
½ cup warm water (105°F to 115°F)
1¼ cups all purpose flour

2 medium eggs, room temperature
¼ cup sour cream, room temperature
Pinch of salt
1½ cups plus 1 tablespoon cake flour

2 medium lemons
4 ounces (¾ cup) blanched almonds, toasted
⅔ cup firmly packed light brown sugar
1½ teaspoons ground cardamom

½ teaspoon cinnamon
¼ teaspoon ground coriander
¼ cup light rum
2 teaspoons vanilla

¾ cup (1½ sticks) butter, room temperature, cut into ¼-inch slices

Topping
5 ounces (1 cup) blanched almonds, toasted
1 cup whipping cream
¾ cup sugar
1 tablespoon unsalted butter
1 teaspoon vanilla
¼ teaspoon almond extract

For brioche: Sprinkle yeast and 1 teaspoon sugar over water in heavy-duty mixer bowl; stir to dissolve. Let stand until foamy, about 10 minutes. Stir in all purpose flour. Cover dough and let rise in warm draft-free area until doubled in volume, about 45 minutes.

Fit mixer with dough hook. Beat eggs, remaining sugar, sour cream and salt into yeast mixture. Add cake flour and beat until dough clings to hook and is shiny and sticky, about 3 minutes. Turn dough out onto floured plastic wrap. Seal and flatten. Freeze 1 hour.

Remove lemon peel (yellow part only) using vegetable peeler. Finely grind peel and almonds with sugar and spices in processor. Transfer mixture to bowl. Add rum and vanilla and stir to form paste. Set almond filling aside.

Grease 14 × 4¼ × 2¾-inch metal loaf pan. Turn dough out onto generously floured surface. Sprinkle dough with flour. Roll dough out into 10 × 15-inch rectangle. Dot half of dough with butter. Spread butter evenly using fingertips. Fold unbuttered half over buttered half. Seal edges tightly. Roll dough out into 10 × 15-inch rectangle. Fold dough into thirds as for business letter. Repeat procedure twice, dusting with flour as necessary. Roll dough out into 14 × 16-inch rectangle. Spread almond filling over dough. Starting at short end, roll dough up as for jelly roll. Place seam side down in prepared pan. Cover dough and let rise in warm draft-free area 30 minutes.

Position rack in center of oven and preheat to 375°F. Line bottom of oven with foil or baking sheet (topping will spatter). Bake brioche 20 minutes.

Meanwhile, prepare topping: Combine almonds, cream, sugar, butter, vanilla and almond extract in heavy medium saucepan and bring to boil over high heat, stirring frequently. Reduce heat to medium-high and cook 15 minutes, stirring frequently. Pour topping over brioche. Bake brioche until topping begins to brown, about 15 minutes. Cool 5 minutes in pan on rack. Run small sharp knife around edges of brioche. Remove brioche from pan and cool slightly on rack.

Glazed Currant Brioche

Should there be any leftovers of this rich yeast bread, they make fabulous French toast.

8 servings

2 envelopes dry yeast
8 tablespoons (½ cup) firmly packed light brown sugar
⅓ cup warm water (105°F to 115°F)

2 cups bread flour
3 eggs
1 teaspoon salt

¾ cup (1½ sticks) unsalted butter, melted (do not boil)
½ cup currants

⅓ cup currant jelly, melted
1 pint strawberries, hulled
Whipped Honey Butter*

Oil large bowl. Grease 6½-cup ring mold. Stir yeast and 1 tablespoon brown sugar into ⅓ cup warm water in small bowl. Let mixture stand until foamy, about 10 minutes.

Insert steel knife in processor. Combine flour, yeast mixture, remaining 7 tablespoons brown sugar, eggs and salt in work bowl. With machine running, pour melted butter through feed tube and process 30 seconds. Add currants and process 3 seconds. Pour into prepared bowl. Cover bowl with plastic wrap. Let rise in warm draft-free area until tripled in volume, about 3 hours.

Punch dough down. Let rise second time in warm draft-free area until doubled in volume, about 1½ hours. Punch dough down again. Cover and refrigerate 4 hours or overnight.

Punch dough down. On well-floured surface, shape into cylinder to fit mold. Arrange in prepared mold, pinching ends together. Cover pan loosely with oiled plastic wrap. Allow to rise in warm draft-free area until dough fills pan, about 1¾ hours.

Position rack in center of oven and preheat to 425°F. Bake brioche 10 minutes. Reduce oven temperature to 350°F and continue baking until golden, about 17 minutes. Invert onto rack. Cool 10 minutes. (*Can be prepared ahead to this point. Cool to room temperature and wrap tightly. Refrigerate up to 3 days or freeze up to 2 months. Bring to room temperature, then wrap loosely in foil. Place in cold oven, set temperature to 350°F and bake brioche until heated through, about 15 minutes.*) Transfer to platter. Brush entire surface of warm brioche with currant jelly. Spoon strawberries into center of ring. Serve warm or at room temperature with Whipped Honey Butter.

*Whipped Honey Butter

Makes about ³/₄ cup

¹/₂ cup (1 stick) **unsalted butter,**
   chilled and cut into 4 pieces

¹/₄ cup **honey**
¹/₄ teaspoon **cinnamon**

Blend butter, honey and cinnamon in processor until smooth, stopping as necessary to scrape down sides, about 1 minute. (*Can be prepared up to 1 week ahead. Cover and refrigerate.*) Serve at room temperature.

Walnut Bread

Makes 1 loaf

Butter
All purpose flour
2¹/₃ cups **all purpose flour**
   1 tablespoon **baking powder**
¹/₂ teaspoon **salt**

⁷/₈ cup **milk**
   1 **egg**
³/₄ cup **sugar**
   6 ounces **walnuts, coarsely chopped**

Preheat oven to 375°F. Butter and flour 9 × 5-inch loaf pan. Sift together 2¹/₃ cups flour, baking powder and salt. Whisk together milk and egg in large bowl. Whisk in sugar. Using wooden spoon, gradually stir in dry ingredients. Fold in walnuts. Turn batter into prepared pan. Bake until tester inserted in center comes out clean, about 50 minutes. Remove from pan. Cool bread completely on rack.

Gruyère-Walnut Loaf

Makes 1 loaf

   1 envelope **dry yeast**
   1 teaspoon **sugar**
 10 tablespoons **warm water (105°F**
   to 115°F)

2³/₄ cups (or more) **unbleached all**
   purpose flour
1¹/₂ teaspoons **salt**
   2 **eggs, room temperature, beaten to**
   blend
   6 tablespoons **vegetable oil**

1¹/₂ cups **grated Gruyère cheese**
   1 cup **walnuts, coarsely chopped**

   1 **egg, room temperature, beaten to**
   blend with pinch of salt (glaze)

Sprinkle yeast and sugar over 4 tablespoons warm water in small bowl; stir to dissolve. Let mixture stand until foamy, about 10 minutes.

Fit processor with steel knife or plastic dough blade. Combine 2³/₄ cups flour and salt in work bowl and mix using on/off turns. Add yeast mixture, 2 eggs and oil. With machine running, pour remaining water through feed tube and process until dough cleans sides of work bowl. If dough sticks to bowl, add more flour through feed tube 1 tablespoon at a time, incorporating each before adding next. Process until smooth and elastic, about 30 seconds. (Dough can also be mixed and kneaded by hand or in mixer.)

Grease large bowl. Add dough to bowl, turning to coat entire surface. Cover bowl with plastic. Let dough rise in warm draft-free area until doubled in volume, about 1¹/₄ hours.

Punch dough down. Knead on lightly floured surface until smooth, about 1 minute. Return dough to bowl, cover with plastic and let rise in warm draft-free area until doubled, about 1 hour.

Grease 9 × 5-inch loaf pan. Knead cheese and walnuts into dough until evenly distributed. Pat dough into 1/2-inch-thick rectangle. Roll up as for jelly roll, starting at 1 short side. Pinch ends to seal. Roll dough over work surface to even. Transfer to prepared pan, arranging seam side down. Cover loaf loosely with damp towel and let rise in warm draft-free area until almost doubled in volume, about 1 hour.

Preheat oven to 375°F. Brush loaf with glaze. Bake until loaf sounds hollow when tapped on bottom, about 40 minutes. Transfer to rack and cool. (*Bread can be prepared 1 day ahead, wrapped tightly and stored at room temperature or frozen up to 2 weeks.*)

Chestnut and Dried Pear Bread

Serve a glass of French pear eau-de-vie with this robust fruit bread.

Makes 1 large loaf

3/4 cup warm water (105°F to 115°F)
1/2 cup firmly packed light brown sugar
2 envelopes dry yeast
1/4 cup (1/2 stick) butter, room temperature
1 egg
1 tablespoon grated orange peel
1 tablespoon grated lemon peel
1 tablespoon cinnamon
2 teaspoons salt
1 teaspoon freshly grated nutmeg

2 cups (about) unbleached all purpose flour
1/2 cup rye flour

12 ounces dried pears
4 ounces dried figs
4 ounces pitted prunes
1 1/2 cups crumbled peeled fresh or vacuum-packed chestnuts
1 cup toasted hazelnuts

1 egg, beaten to blend (glaze)

Grease large bowl. Combine water, sugar and yeast in processor. Mix in butter, egg, orange and lemon peel, cinnamon, salt and nutmeg. Add 1 cup all purpose flour and rye flour and process until smooth. Let stand 1 minute. With machine running, gradually add enough all purpose flour through feed tube to form moist dough that pulls away from sides of bowl. Continue processing until smooth and elastic, about 40 seconds.

Transfer dough to prepared bowl, turning to coat entire surface. Cover bowl with damp towel. Let dough rise in warm draft-free area until doubled in volume, about 1 1/4 hours.

Grease baking sheet. Cut dried fruit into 1/2-inch dice. Combine with chestnuts and hazelnuts. Punch dough down. Knead in fruit and nut mixture. Flatten dough into 12-inch-long rectangle. Roll up into log, starting at one 12-inch side. Transfer to prepared sheet, arranging seam side down. Cover with damp towel. Let dough rise in warm draft-free area until almost doubled in volume, about 1 hour.

Preheat oven to 350°F. Brush bread with glaze. Bake until golden brown and firm to touch, about 1 hour. Cool completely on rack before serving.

8 ❧ Desserts

To the traditionalist, the typical French dessert must be a simple apple tart topped with crème fraîche, or a wedge of cheese to eat with fruit and a glass of good brandy or eau-de-vie. But how can anyone ignore the extraordinary temptations of the *patisserie* windows in every town, where such treats as Breton shortbread, flaky puff pastries, syrupy rum babas and intensely rich chocolate truffles beckon?

In this chapter you can sample delicious country desserts from all over France, from the traditionalist's Fresh Peach Tart (page 101), Flagnarde custard (page 105) which is eaten with fruit preserves, and Little Prune Turnovers (page 97), custard-topped crepes filled with rum-soaked fruit. For the more impressive finale, try La Mystère (page 109), rich vanilla ice cream topped with chestnuts and chocolate syrup, whipped cream and almonds; Applejack Cake Filled with Candied Apples (page 111), a génoise box filled and topped with whipped cream and apples; or delicate Individual Nut Meringue Cakes filled with Chocolate Whipped Cream and dusted with powdered sugar (page 113).

In keeping with tradition, finish off your meal with a *digestif* glass of brandy, such as Cognac, Armagnac or marc; or a French fruit brandy or liqueur such as Calvados, made from apples; kirsch, distilled from cherries; poire William, made from pears; or framboise, from raspberries.

 Fruit Desserts

Ragout of Dried Fruits

Any combination of dried fruits can be used in this tasty compote.

6 servings

1 pound dried fruits (such as apricots, peaches, pears, prunes, cherries)
1 750-ml bottle Moscato or other dessert wine

3 tablespoons honey
7 teaspoons fresh lemon juice
Pinch of salt
Julienne of lemon peel (optional)

Combine fruits, wine and honey in heavy large saucepan. Bring to boil. Reduce heat and simmer until fruit is tender, stirring occasionally, about 15 minutes. Cool. Mix in lemon juice and salt. Refrigerate at least 2 hours. (*Can be prepared 1 day ahead.*) Let stand at room temperature 20 minutes before serving. Garnish with lemon peel.

Wine- and Ginger-marinated Fruit

6 servings

8 cups bite-size pieces of fruit (combination of orange sections, banana slices, red and green seedless grapes, strawberries and unpeeled Granny Smith and Red Delicious apple slices)

1½ cups water
¾ cup sugar
1 cup dry white wine
2 teaspoons grated peeled fresh ginger

Combine fruit in large bowl and mix gently.

Cook water and sugar in heavy medium saucepan over low heat, swirling pan occasionally, until sugar dissolves. Increase heat and boil 5 minutes. Add wine and ginger and cook until heated through. Pour over fruit and serve.

Fruit Salad with Bachelor's Confiture

4 servings

4½ cups fresh fruit (any combination of sliced peaches, apricots, plums and figs, cubed apples and pears, or whole raspberries, straw-berries, cherries, grapes, currants or prunes)

½ cup sugar
1 cup Bachelor's Confiture*
Walnut Bread (see page 93)

Mix fruit and sugar in large bowl. Stir in confiture. Cover and chill 1 hour. Serve with thin slices of Walnut Bread.

*Bachelor's Confiture

This combination of seasonal fruit soaked in vodka and sugar should mellow for at least two months for maximum flavor. As you use the confiture, add more fruit, vodka and sugar to keep a steady supply.

Makes about 2 pounds

2 pounds peaches, plums, apricots, prunes, pears, apples, figs, strawberries, raspberries, cherries, grapes and currants or any combination

1 750-ml bottle (or more) vodka
2 pounds sugar
1 large lemon, cut into ⅛-inch slices

Peel and pit peaches; cut into eighths. Pit plums, apricots and prunes; cut into sixths. Halve and core pears and apples; cut into eighths. Halve figs. Leave remaining fruit whole.

Pour vodka into large glass jar with lid. Add sugar and stir to dissolve. Add fruit. Pour in more vodka if necessary to cover fruit completely. Let stand in cool dry place at least 2 months, stirring occasionally and adding more vodka, fruit, sugar and lemon as desired to replenish supply.

Little Prune Turnovers

8 servings

32 pitted prunes
½ cup dark rum

1 cup sifted all purpose flour
3 eggs, room temperature
1 teaspoon grated lemon peel
½ cup apple cider
½ cup half and half
2 tablespoons powdered sugar
Pinch of salt

1 cup whipping cream
½ cup milk
6 egg yolks
⅓ cup firmly packed light brown sugar

¼ cup (½ stick) butter, melted

Soak prunes in rum 24 hours. Drain prunes, reserving any liquid.

Whisk flour, eggs and lemon peel in large bowl. Gradually beat in cider and half and half. Stir in powdered sugar, salt and any prune liquid. Let stand at room temperature at least 20 minutes. Strain batter into bowl.

Scald whipping cream with milk in heavy large saucepan. Whisk yolks and brown sugar in large bowl, then gradually whisk in hot cream mixture. Pour mixture back into pan. Cook over medium-low heat, stirring constantly with wooden spoon, until foam disappears from surface and mixture leaves path on back of spoon when finger is drawn across; *do not boil*. Strain through fine sieve into bowl. Whisk custard to cool quickly. (*Can be prepared several hours ahead, covered and kept at room temperature.*)

Heat 5-inch crepe pan or heavy skillet over medium-high heat. Grease with paper towels soaked in melted butter. Remove from heat. Working quickly, add about 2 tablespoons batter to pan, tilting until bottom is covered with thin layer of batter. Pour any excess batter back into bowl. Cook crepe until bottom is very lightly browned, loosening edges with knife. Turn crepe over and cook second side. Remove pan from heat. Place 2 prunes in center of crepe. Lightly brush some uncooked batter along half of crepe border. Fold other half of crepe over prunes. Return pan to heat and press two edges together for several seconds to seal. Transfer turnover to warm platter. Repeat with remaining batter and prunes. (*Can be prepared several hours ahead. Cover with foil and reheat in 425°F oven 5 minutes.*) Spoon some custard atop turnovers and serve immediately. Pass remaining custard separately.

Strawberry Delights

Makes 8

Puff Pastry
1¹/₂ cups all purpose flour
¹/₂ cup cake flour
¹/₂ teaspoon salt
1 cup (2 sticks) unsalted butter,
    very well chilled
¹/₂ cup water

Strawberries
2 cups very small strawberries (or
    halved, if large)
¹/₃ cup sugar
1 teaspoon raspberry liqueur

Pastry Cream
¹/₃ cup sugar
1¹/₂ tablespoons all purpose flour,
    sifted
1¹/₂ tablespoons cornstarch, sifted
1 cup milk
2 egg yolks, beaten to blend

¹/₄ cup (¹/₂ stick) unsalted butter,
    room temperature
1 tablespoon raspberry liqueur

Strawberry Coulis
¹/₂ cup sugar
¹/₂ cup water
1¹/₂ cups fresh strawberry puree
1 tablespoon raspberry liqueur
1 teaspoon fresh lemon juice

Cream Cheese Topping
¹/₂ cup whipping cream
4 ounces cream cheese
2 tablespoons sugar
    Few drops of raspberry liqueur

1 egg yolk blended with
    ¹/₂ tablespoon water (glaze)

¹/₂ cup red currant jelly, melted

For pastry: Combine flours and salt in bowl. Set ¹/₄ cup of mixture aside. Cut 4 tablespoons butter into remainder until mixture resembles coarse meal. Mound on surface; make large well in center. Add water to well. With one hand, quickly incorporate flour into water; do not overwork. Gather dough into rough mass. Cut through mass several times with pastry cutter until dough just starts to bind together. Wrap in plastic; chill 30 minutes.

Knead remaining ³/₄ cup butter and reserved ¹/₄ cup flour mixture until same consistency as dough. Shape into 5-inch round and wrap in waxed paper. Refrigerate 30 minutes.

Roll dough out on lightly floured surface into 12-inch circle. Place butter in center of dough. Fold dough over to encase butter completely. Turn dough over. Roll package out gently and evenly into 8 × 18-inch rectangle; do not roll over edges. Fold dough over into 3 equal sections as for business letter. Press edges down lightly with rolling pin to seal. (This is 1 turn.)

Give dough a quarter turn so it opens like a book. Roll again into 8 × 18-inch rectangle. Fold into thirds. (This is second turn.) Wrap in waxed paper, then plastic, and refrigerate at least 1 hour. Give dough 2 more turns; refrigerate at least 2 hours or overnight. Give dough last 2 turns (for total of 6) and refrigerate at least 2 hours before rolling and cutting. (*Can be prepared up to 3 days ahead, wrapped and refrigerated.*)

Roll dough out on lightly floured surface into square ¹/₂ to ³/₄ inch thick. Set on baking sheet and freeze 20 minutes. Trim sides of dough. Cut into 4 strips about 4 inches wide. Freeze until firm. Cut each strip into two 4-inch squares. Freeze at least 30 minutes.

For strawberries: Mix berries, sugar and liqueur. Chill at least 1 hour.

For pastry cream: Combine sugar, flour and cornstarch in medium bowl. Bring milk to rolling boil. Whisk half of milk into sugar mixture. Whisk in yolks until smooth. Reboil remaining milk. Whisk sugar mixture into milk until very thick, about 30 seconds. Remove from heat and whisk until cool. Whisk in butter 1 tablespoon at a time. Blend in liqueur. Cover with plastic and refrigerate until ready to use. (*Can be prepared up to 1 day ahead.*)

For coulis: Cook sugar and water in heavy small saucepan over low heat until sugar dissolves, swirling pan occasionally. Increase heat and boil 4 minutes or until candy thermometer registers 200°F. Cool. Drain liquid from whole strawberries into heavy small saucepan. Boil until candy thermometer registers 200°F. Blend strawberry syrup into strawberry puree. Add sugar syrup to puree to desired sweetness (be sure to oversweeten; coulis will lose sweetness after refrigeration). Blend in liqueur and lemon juice. Refrigerate until ready to use. (*Can be prepared up to 1 day ahead, covered and refrigerated.*)

For topping: Gradually beat cream into cream cheese in bowl of heavy-duty mixer at medium speed until semifirm, about 10 minutes. Blend in sugar and liqueur. Refrigerate until ready to use. (*Can be prepared up to 1 day ahead.*)

Preheat oven to 425°F. Brush egg glaze over pastry squares. Arrange on large baking sheet. Bake 20 minutes (if tops brown too quickly, cover loosely with foil). Split each square in half horizontally. Return to oven cut side up and bake until insides are dry, 3 minutes.

To assemble: Fill 8 halves with pastry cream. Cover with remaining 8 halves. Brush tops lightly with melted currant jelly. Arrange whole strawberries over. Brush strawberries with jelly to glaze.

Spoon 3 tablespoons strawberry coulis into each of 8 dessert plates. Place pastry in center. Quarter any remaining whole strawberries and arrange around pastry in coulis. Pass cream cheese topping separately.

Cream Cheese with Pear and Cider Butter

Serve for brunch, lunch or as an unusual fruit and cheese course.

12 to 14 servings

Pear Cider Butter
 2 **pounds ripe bartlett pears, peeled, cored and pureed**
 2 **quarts sweet or hard cider**
 6 **tablespoons cider vinegar**
 ¹/₂ **cup (1 stick) unsalted butter, chopped**

Cream Cheese
 ¹/₂ **pound small curd cottage cheese**
 ¹/₂ **pound cream cheese (preferably fresh), room temperature**
 ¹/₂ **cup plain yogurt**
 2 **cups whipping cream**

For pear butter: Combine pear puree, cider and vinegar in heavy large saucepan over medium heat. Cook until reduced to 2¹/₂ cups, about 1¹/₄ hours, stirring frequently and reducing heat at end to prevent burning. Strain through fine sieve. Return puree to saucepan. Bring to full boil over medium heat. Whisk in butter. Pour into bowl. Refrigerate until well chilled. (*Can be prepared several days ahead.*)

For cream cheese: Mix cottage cheese in blender or processor until smooth. Beat cream cheese in large bowl until light. Beat in cottage cheese, 1 tablespoon at a time. Blend in yogurt until light. Whip cream in another large bowl until very stiff. Fold into cheese mixture. Spoon mixture into perforated cheese mold or colander lined with large piece of dampened cheesecloth. Fold cloth over top. Place mold over deep bowl to allow whey to drain. Refrigerate cream cheese mixture overnight.

To serve, unmold cheese onto dessert platter. Surround cheese with pear butter or pass separately.

Tarts, Pastries and Confections

Apple Clafouti à la Ritz

This delicious dessert was inspired by a creation of chef Guy Legay at the Hôtel Ritz in Paris.

8 servings

4 medium Granny Smith apples (1³/₄ pounds total), peeled, halved lengthwise and cored
¹/₄ cup (¹/₂ stick) unsalted butter
3 tablespoons sugar

³/₄ cup crème fraîche
¹/₄ cup whipping cream

¹/₄ cup sugar
1 egg
2 teaspoons vanilla
¹/₄ teaspoon freshly grated nutmeg
1 baked Butter Pastry Crust*
    Additional crème fraîche

Position rack in center of oven and then preheat to 375°F.

Insert thick slicer in processor. Stand apples in feed tube and slice using firm pressure. (Apples should be about ¹/₄ inch thick.) Melt butter in heavy 12-inch skillet over medium heat. Add apples and 3 tablespoons sugar and cook until tender, turning occasionally with spatula, about 12 minutes. (*Apple mixture can be prepared 4 hours ahead. Let stand at room temperature.*)

Blend ³/₄ cup crème fraîche, cream, ¹/₄ cup sugar, egg, vanilla and nutmeg in processor using 5 on/off turns. Arrange apples in crust in pan. Pour custard over. Place pan on baking sheet. Bake until custard is firm when tart is shaken, about 30 minutes. (*Can be prepared 4 hours ahead. Let stand at room temperature. Place tart in cold oven, turn temperature to 300°F and rewarm 15 minutes.*) Serve warm with crème fraîche.

*Butter Pastry Crust

Makes one 11-inch crust

¹/₂ cup (1 stick) well-chilled unsalted butter, cut into 8 pieces
5 tablespoons ice water

1 tablespoon sugar
¹/₂ teaspoon salt
1 cup unbleached all purpose flour

Chop butter in processor using 6 on/off turns. Add water, sugar and salt and blend 5 seconds. Add flour and process just until combined; do not form ball. Place dough in plastic bag and seal. Working through bag, flatten into disc. Refrigerate at least 2 hours. (*Can be prepared ahead and refrigerated overnight or frozen up to 3 months.*)

Roll dough out on lightly floured surface to ¹/₈-inch-thick circle. Press into 11-inch round tart pan with removable bottom. Trim dough, leaving 1-inch overlap; reserve trimmings. Fold in overlap to form double-thick sides. Press dough firmly in place, pushing ¹/₄ inch above edge of pan. Pinch dough to form decorative edge. Pierce bottom and sides with fork. Refrigerate pastry for 30 minutes.

Position rack in center of oven and preheat to 400°F. Line pastry with parchment or foil and fill with dried beans or rice. Bake 12 minutes. Remove paper and beans. Pierce pastry again. Bake until light brown, about 18 minutes. Transfer pastry to rack. Repair any cracks in crust by smoothing in reserved dough. Cool completely.

Caramelized Fig Tart

8 servings

1½ cups sifted all purpose flour
1 tablespoon superfine sugar
½ teaspoon salt
½ teaspoon cinnamon
½ teaspoon finely grated lemon peel
9 tablespoons unsalted butter, cut into tablespoons, room temperature
1 egg, beaten to blend

Superfine sugar

24 canned Kadota figs

Whipped cream flavored with powdered sugar and finely grated lemon peel (optional)

Combine flour, sugar, salt, cinnamon and grated lemon peel in processor. Blend in 7 tablespoons butter using on/off turns until mixture resembles coarse meal. With machine running, add beaten egg through feed tube in slow steady stream, mixing just until dough comes together; do not form ball (entire egg may not be necessary). Flatten dough into disc ½ inch high. Wrap in waxed paper and chill at least 1 hour.

Coat 9- to 10-inch tart pan with removable bottom with remaining 2 tablespoons butter. Sprinkle bottom and sides with sugar. Roll dough out on lightly floured surface to thickness of ⅙ inch. Fit into pan; trim and form edges. Refrigerate pastry shell 30 minutes.

Position rack in bottom of oven and preheat to 400°F. Drain figs thoroughly, reserving syrup. Pat figs dry; cut in half. Arrange halves seed side up in concentric circles in pastry shell. Bake 30 minutes. Remove tart from oven. Reposition rack in top of oven.

Cook syrup over high heat until reduced to ⅓ cup. Brush figs and rim of crust with syrup. Continue baking until figs and crust are caramelized, 15 to 20 minutes. Immediately remove tart from pan and slide carefully onto lightly buttered rack. Let cool. Serve with whipped cream if desired.

Fresh Peach Tart

6 servings

Pastry
1¾ cups unbleached all purpose flour
9 tablespoons well-chilled butter, cut into small pieces
⅓ cup sugar
4 egg yolks
1½ teaspoons finely grated lemon peel
½ teaspoon vanilla
¼ teaspoon salt

Filling
1 cup plain yogurt
3 to 4 tablespoons firmly packed light brown sugar
½ teaspoon vanilla
½ cup whipping cream

3 small ripe peaches, peeled
¼ cup fresh red currants or fresh berries

For pastry: Butter six 4½-inch tart pans with removable bottoms. Mound flour on work surface. Make well in center. Add butter, sugar, yolks, peel, vanilla and salt to well. Using fingertips, mix until sugar and salt dissolve. Gradually incorporate flour into butter mixture until dough is crumbly. Using heel of hand, push small pieces of dough away from you to blend butter and flour thoroughly. (Or, mix all ingredients in processor until dough comes together, 30 to 45 seconds.)

Gather dough into ball. Divide into 6 pieces. Press each piece into prepared pan; dough should be about ¼ inch thick. Pierce dough. Refrigerate shells until firm, about 30 minutes.

Preheat oven to 375°F. Bake shells until golden brown, 20 to 25 minutes. Cool completely in pans on rack.

For filling: Mix yogurt, brown sugar and vanilla in medium bowl. Beat cream in another bowl until soft peaks form. Fold cream into yogurt mixture.

To assemble: Remove tart shells from pans. Set each shell on plate. Halve peaches; remove pits. Cut each half into 6 slices. Spoon filling into each shell. Arrange 6 peach slices decoratively atop each. Garnish with currants or berries. Serve immediately.

Sugar Tart with Plum Compote

Italian prune plums add color to this irresistible country dessert.

6 to 8 servings

Plum Compote
1 pound ripe Italian prune plums,* pitted
⅓ cup honey
⅓ teaspoon finely grated lemon peel

Sucrette
2 cups sifted all purpose flour
1 tablespoon cornstarch
¾ cup warm milk (105°F to 115°F)
2 tablespoons honey
1 envelope dry yeast

6 tablespoons (¾ stick) butter, melted and cooled
½ teaspoon salt

8 tablespoons (1 stick) unsalted butter, room temperature

⅓ cup sugar
2 tablespoons whipping cream
½ teaspoon orange flower water
⅓ teaspoon finely grated lemon peel
⅓ teaspoon ground cardamom

For compote: Cook plums, honey and peel in heavy large saucepan over medium heat until plums are very tender and thick syrup forms, stirring frequently (time will vary depending on ripeness of plums). Transfer to glass bowl. Refrigerate until well chilled.

For sucrette: Resift flour with cornstarch into large bowl. Make well in center. Add milk, honey and yeast to well. Mix ¼ of flour mixture into well and let stand until bubbly, about 10 minutes. Add 6 tablespoons melted butter and ½ teaspoon salt to well. Gradually draw flour from inner edge of well into center until all flour is incorporated. Beat with wooden spoon or knead until smooth and elastic, about 5 minutes. Cover and let rise in warm draft-free area until doubled in volume, about 30 minutes.

Coat 9-inch nonmetal pie plate with 1 tablespoon butter. Spread dough evenly on bottom of plate. Cover and let rise in warm draft-free area until doubled in volume, about 25 minutes.

Cream remaining 7 tablespoons butter with remaining ingredients. Spread evenly over dough; dough will deflate. Cover and let rise in warm draft-free area until doubled, about 20 minutes.

Preheat oven to 375°F. Bake sucrette until golden brown, 25 to 30 minutes. Cool to lukewarm in plate. Cut into slices. Spoon plums over and serve.

*If unavailable, an equal amount of canned whole purple plums in syrup can be substituted. Drain plums, reserving liquid. Cook liquid with honey and peel until thickened. Add plums and heat gently.

Apple Sauce Fritters

For these unique fritters, a yeast puff pastry is filled with apple marmalade, deep fried and dusted with powdered sugar.

Makes about 40

Dough

4½ cups sifted all purpose flour
1 cup milk, scalded and cooled to 105°F to 115°F
1½ teaspoons dry yeast
3 tablespoons sugar
1 egg
1 teaspoon finely grated lemon peel
½ teaspoon cinnamon

1 cup (2 sticks) butter, well chilled

Apple Filling

3½ pounds tart green apples, peeled and thinly sliced
½ cup sugar
1 teaspoon cinnamon
½ teaspoon finely grated lemon peel
1 tablespoon butter

1 egg, beaten to blend

Oil (for deep frying)
Powdered sugar

For dough: Sift flour onto work suface and make well in center. Add milk and yeast, stirring with fingertips until yeast dissolves. Whisk sugar and egg in small bowl until slowly dissolving ribbon forms when whisk is lifted. When yeast bubbles, blend sugar mixture, lemon peel and cinnamon into well. Starting from outside of well, gradually incorporate flour into liquid. Form dough into ball. Knead until smooth, about 10 minutes. Flatten into ½-inch round. Wrap in plastic and refrigerate at least 1 hour.

Knead butter until same consistency as dough. Shape into round ½ inch thick. Roll dough out on lightly floured surface into round twice as wide as butter. Place butter in center of dough. Fold dough over to encase butter completely. Wrap in plastic and refrigerate for 30 minutes.

Roll dough package out gently and evenly on lightly floured work surface into 8 × 24-inch rectangle ½ inch thick; do not roll over edges. Fold dough into 3 equal sections as for business letter. Press edges down lightly with rolling pin to seal. (This is 1 turn.) Give dough a quarter turn so it opens like a book. Roll again into 8 × 24-inch rectangle ½ inch thick. Fold into thirds. (This is second turn.) Wrap in plastic and refrigerate 30 minutes. Repeat sequence twice for a total of 6 turns, wrapping dough in plastic and chilling 30 minutes between every 2 turns. If dough is hard to roll, chill longer between turns to relax dough.

Meanwhile, prepare filling: Cook apples, sugar, cinnamon and lemon peel in heavy large saucepan over low heat until almost reduced to paste, stirring occasionally, about 2 hours. Blend in butter. Cool to room temperature.

Lightly flour baking sheets. Roll dough out on generously floured surface into large square ⅙ inch thick. Cut dough into circles using 2- to 2½-inch cutter. Gather scraps and refrigerate 30 minutes. Reroll and cut additional circles. Set 1 teaspoon apple filling in center of 1 round. Brush edge with beaten egg. Top with second round. Seal edges with fork tines. Repeat with remaining circles and filling. Arrange on prepared sheets. Cover with plastic wrap and refrigerate 45 minutes. (*Can be prepared 1 day ahead.*)

Heat oil in deep fryer or heavy large saucepan to 400°F. Fry fritters until golden, about 4 minutes. Drain on paper towels. Sift powdered sugar over tops. Serve immediately.

Shortbread Brittany Style

Serve with Coupes Plougastel (page 109).

Makes about 80

1¼ cups (2½ sticks) butter, room temperature
1 teaspoon ground cardamom
1 teaspoon orange flower water
1 cup sugar
2½ cups sifted all purpose flour
¼ cup cornstarch
Pinch of salt

1 egg yolk
3 tablespoons whipping cream

Cream butter in large bowl of electric mixer. Beat in cardamom and orange flower water. Stir in sugar, using rubber spatula, just until incorporated. Combine flour, cornstarch and salt. Fold into butter mixture until ball forms. Set dough on 14 × 16-inch piece of plastic wrap. Cover with second piece of plastic wrap. Roll dough out ¼ inch thick. Refrigerate 1 hour.

Preheat oven to 375°F. Cut chilled dough into cookies using 1½-inch round cutter (return scraps to refrigerator to firm). Arrange cookies on heavy baking sheets, spacing 1½ inches apart. Blend yolk and cream. Brush thinly on each cookie. Trace crisscross pattern on top of each, using fork tines. Bake until golden brown, about 7 minutes. Transfer to wire rack and cool completely. Repeat rolling, cutting and baking shortbread with chilled scraps. Store cookies in airtight container.

Spiced Madeleines

Makes about 2½ dozen

1 cup all purpose flour
½ teaspoon baking powder
½ teaspoon cardamom seeds, crushed in mortar with pestle
½ teaspoon grated nutmeg
¼ teaspoon ground allspice

3 eggs, room temperature
⅔ cup sugar
1 teaspoon vanilla
10 tablespoons (1¼ sticks) unsalted butter, melted and cooled

Position rack in center of oven and preheat to 400°F. Generously butter 36 madeleine molds. Combine first 5 ingredients in medium bowl. In top of double boiler, stir eggs over barely simmering water until just tepid. Transfer to bowl of electric mixer. Gradually beat in sugar. Continue beating until mixture is pale yellow and triples in volume. Sift half of dry ingredients over eggs and gently fold in. Repeat with remaining dry ingredients. Fold in vanilla. Gently fold in butter in 3 additions. Spoon batter into molds, filling ¾ full. Bake until cookies are golden brown, 10 to 15 minutes. Serve warm or at room temperature.

add ¼ c. cocoa

Savoie-style Chocolate Truffles

Makes about 4 dozen

½ cup sugar
¼ cup water
⅓ cup toasted hazelnuts, husked

7 ounces bittersweet or semisweet chocolate
1 ounce unsweetened chocolate

¼ cup (½ stick) unsalted butter
½ cup whipping cream
Pinch of salt
1½ tablespoons green Chartreuse liqueur or dark rum

Unsweetened cocoa powder

Butter baking sheets. Stir sugar and water in heavy 9-inch skillet until sugar dissolves. Place over medium-high heat and bring to boil without stirring. Let boil until mixture registers 305°F (hard-crack stage) on candy thermometer, washing down sides of pan with wet brush to prevent crystallization. Reduce heat to low, add hazelnuts and stir until sugar turns deep brown. Pour mixture onto prepared sheets. Cool completely. Break into pieces. Mix in processor to coarse powder using on/off turns (hazelnut pieces should be about ⅙ inch).

Melt chocolates and butter in top of double boiler set over hot water. Scald cream and salt in heavy small saucepan. Whisk cream into chocolate by teaspoonfuls until mixture is smooth. Remove from heat and cool slightly. Stir in hazelnut praline. Gradually blend in Chartreuse. Cool completely. Cover and refrigerate overnight.

Spread cocoa powder evenly on waxed paper. Scoop out 1-inch pieces of chocolate mixture with melon baller or teaspoon and roll into smooth rounds. Toss each in cocoa powder, shaking off excess. Arrange on plate. Refrigerate. Let stand at room temperature about 15 minutes before serving.

❦ *Puddings, Soufflés and Ices*

Flagnarde

This fruity, firm-textured custard makes a comforting finale to any meal.

6 servings

¾ cup raisins
1½ tablespoons brandy

1⅓ cups milk
1 vanilla bean, split

4 eggs, room temperature
½ cup sugar

¾ cup all purpose flour
¼ teaspoon salt

Powdered sugar
Strawberry preserves

Marinate raisins in brandy in small bowl at least 30 minutes.

Bring milk and vanilla bean to boil in heavy medium saucepan. Remove from heat and let steep 5 minutes.

Preheat oven to 375°F. Butter 6-cup shallow baking dish. Beat eggs and sugar in large bowl until thick and pale. Whisk in flour 1 tablespoon at a time. Remove vanilla bean from milk. Whisk milk into batter. Blend in salt. Stir in undrained raisins. Pour batter into prepared dish. Bake until puffy and golden brown, about 20 minutes. Sprinkle with powdered sugar. Serve immediately with preserves.

Rich Rice Pudding with Poached Pears and Marmalade Sauce

4 servings

Pudding
½ cup pearl (short-grain) rice

3 cups milk
1 vanilla bean, split lengthwise
1 tablespoon grated orange peel
2 teaspoons grated lemon peel
  Salt

5 tablespoons sugar
2 egg yolks
2 tablespoons (¼ stick) unsalted
  butter

Pears
3 cups water
1 cup sugar
2 cinnamon sticks
6 whole cloves
2 large Bosc pears, peeled, cored
  and cut lengthwise into sixths

½ cup orange marmalade

1 3½ × ⅛-inch piece candied
  angelica

For pudding: Blanch rice in large pot of boiling water 2 minutes; drain well.

Scald milk with vanilla bean and citrus peels in heavy medium saucepan over medium-high heat. Reduce heat to low. Remove vanilla bean. Stir rice and large pinch of salt into saucepan. Cover and simmer 50 minutes, stirring occasionally to prevent sticking.

Uncover saucepan. Stir rice until all milk is absorbed, 5 to 8 minutes. Add sugar and yolks and stir until mixture thickens slightly, about 5 minutes. Remove from heat. Add butter and stir until melted. (*Can be prepared 1 day ahead. Cool completely; refrigerate. Bring to room temperature before using.*)

For pears: Cook water, sugar, cinnamon and cloves in heavy medium saucepan over low heat until sugar dissolves, swirling pan occasionally. Bring to boil. Add pears. Reduce heat and simmer until tender but not mushy, about 5 minutes (time will vary depending on ripeness of pears). Drain, reserving liquid.

For sauce: Place marmalade in heavy small saucepan. Whisk in enough pear liquid (2 to 3 tablespoons) to loosen. Cook over low heat until warmed through, about 5 minutes.

To assemble: Cut angelica into 12 triangles measuring ¼ inch at base and 6 triangles measuring ½ inch at base. Turn pudding onto large platter. Smooth top and sides; pudding should be about ½ inch high. With narrow ends facing inward, arrange 6 pear sections over pudding in spoke pattern, leaving space between pears and in center. Spoon sauce into center. Brush pears lightly with sauce. Set large angelica triangles with single points facing outward between tops of pears. Set small angelica triangles with single points facing inward between bottoms of pears. Spoon remaining sauce around pudding. Arrange remaining pears atop sauce and serve.

Cognac Crème Anglaise

Serve this elegant sauce with pound cake, fruitcake, chocolate cake, poached fruit or fresh berries. Or use as a topping for molded creams or puddings.

Makes about 2¼ cups

6 egg yolks, room temperature
⅓ cup firmly packed light brown
  sugar

Pinch of salt
2 cups half and half
¼ cup Cognac

Whisk yolks, sugar and salt in heavy medium saucepan. Slowly whisk in half and half. Stir over medium heat using wooden spoon until custard thickens and leaves path when finger is drawn across spoon; do not boil. Strain into bowl. Cool. Mix in Cognac. Serve warm or at room temperature. (*Can be prepared 2 days ahead. Cover tightly and refrigerate. To rewarm, heat in top of double boiler over simmering water, stirring frequently.*)

🍒 *Sweet Soufflés*

There are not many desserts that can match the drama of a glorious soufflé. Its impressive appearance and unique delicate texture make for a showstopper finale that belies the simple preparation. Keep the following tips in mind, and you'll see how foolproof soufflés really are.

- Make sure there is ample room for soufflé to rise without touching top of oven; if not, position rack in lower third of oven instead of center.
- Preheat oven 15 to 20 minutes.
- To ensure even heat, do not bake other things at the same time as soufflé.
- Generally it is most convenient to prepare soufflé base ahead and bake just before serving. If preparing just before baking, preheat oven and butter dish before beginning base.
- Experts think that an egg is easier to separate when cold because fat in yolk is firmer and yolk is less likely to break. Separate eggs directly from refrigerator; bring to room temperature while readying other ingredients.
- Always use clean, dry mixing bowl and beaters for egg whites.
- Beat whites carefully. If overbeaten, they will become lumpy and will not blend into mixture. If underbeaten, they will not be firm enough to support soufflé and make it rise.
- Gently fold whites into base as soon as they are beaten or they will deflate.
- To fold, move a medium or large rubber spatula under mixture in a clockwise direction and bring base mixture up over whites, simultaneously rotating bowl counterclockwise. Repeat this motion several times until batter is just blended. A few very small streaks of white may remain.

Basic Sweet Soufflé

4 servings

1 cup milk
1/2 large or 1 medium vanilla bean, split lengthwise

Flavoring (see Variations)

3 egg yolks, room temperature
3 tablespoons sugar
1/4 cup all purpose flour

5 egg whites, room temperature
Pinch of cream of tartar
2 tablespoons sugar
Powdered sugar

Bring milk to boil with vanilla bean in heavy small saucepan. Remove from heat, cover and let steep 30 minutes.

Prepare flavoring (see Variations).

Remove vanilla bean from milk; reserve for another use. Return milk to boil. Remove from heat. Whisk yolks and 3 tablespoons sugar in medium bowl until creamy, about 1 minute. Add flour to yolks and whisk until just blended. Gradually whisk in hot milk. Return mixture to saucepan. Whisk over medium-low heat until very thick, about 3 minutes. Remove custard from heat. Gradually blend in flavoring. Scrape custard down and inward from sides of pan. Cool until just warm to touch. (*Can be prepared 1 day ahead. Press piece of plastic onto surface of custard. Refrigerate if making more than 4 hours ahead. Before continuing with recipe, whisk over low heat until barely warm. Do not let custard boil.*)

Position rack in center of oven and preheat to 400°F. Generously butter 6- to 7-cup soufflé dish. Coat with sugar. Using electric mixer, beat whites with cream of tartar to soft peaks. Gradually add 2 tablespoons sugar and beat until stiff but not dry. Whisk custard until smooth. Fold 1/4 of whites into custard to lighten; gently pour custard over remaining whites and fold together. Pour into prepared dish, spreading evenly. Bake soufflé until puffed and almost firm to touch, 20 to 25 minutes. Dust with sugar.

Variations

Chocolate: Melt 4 ounces bittersweet (not unsweetened) or semisweet chocolate in double boiler over simmering water. Cool to room temperature before blending into cooked custard.

Coffee: Dissolve 4 teaspoons instant coffee crystals in 2 tablespoons hot water. Cool to room temperature before blending into cooked custard.

Orange: Mix 1 tablespoon grated orange peel and 2 tablespoons fresh orange juice into cooked custard. Add 1 tablespoon Grand Marnier to custard just before adding egg whites.

Lemon: Mix 3 tablespoons fresh lemon juice with 1 tablespoon powdered sugar and whisk into cooked custard with 1 tablespoon grated lemon peel.

Spirits: When making custard, substitute 14 tablespoons milk plus 2 tablespoons Grand Marnier, kirsch, pear eau-de-vie or framboise (raspberry eau-de-vie) for 1 cup milk. Blend 3 tablespoons of same spirit into custard just before adding egg whites.

Soft Peach Mousse with Raspberry Sauce and Fresh Currants

This can be made ahead and frozen. Thaw it completely before serving.

6 servings

Raspberry Sauce
1 **10-ounce package frozen sweetened raspberries, thawed (undrained)**

Peach Mousse
6 **large peaches, nectarines or combination (2 1/3 pounds total)**

2 **tablespoons fresh lime juice**
1/2 **cup sugar**
3 **egg whites**

1/2 **cup fresh red currants (optional)**

For sauce: Blend raspberries in processor until smooth, about 1 minute. Strain into small bowl. (*Can be prepared 3 days ahead and refrigerated.*)

For mousse: Peel and quarter 3 peaches.

Puree peeled peaches with 1 tablespoon lime juice and 1/4 cup sugar in processor. Measure 1 cup to use in mousse.

Using electric mixer, beat whites until soft peaks form. Add remaining 1/4 cup sugar 1 tablespoon at a time, beating until thick and glossy. Gently fold puree into whites. Divide among 6 shallow dessert bowls, smoothing tops. (*Can be prepared 2 days ahead and frozen. Before serving, let stand at room temperature until thawed, about 3 hours.*)

Peel remaining 3 peaches and slice. Mix with remaining 1 tablespoon lime juice in medium bowl. Let stand 5 minutes. Gently fold each mousse to recombine. Pat peaches dry with paper towels. Arrange atop desserts in spoke pattern. Spoon 2 tablespoons raspberry sauce around outer edge of each and 1/2 teaspoon in center. Garnish with currants and serve.

Coupes Plougastel

6 servings

Vanilla Ice Cream
- 16 egg yolks
- ²/₃ cup sugar
- 1 quart milk, scalded with seeds from 1 vanilla bean
  Pinch of salt
- 3 tablespoons vanilla

Strawberry Sherbet
- 1 pound fresh or unsweetened frozen strawberries, crushed

- 24 ounces strawberry jam, melted
- 3¹/₂ tablespoons fresh lemon juice
  Pinch of salt

- 1 cup whole strawberries
- 1 cup thinly sliced strawberries
- 1 tablespoon red wine vinegar
  Powdered sugar

  Fresh mint or basil leaves

For ice cream: Mix yolks and sugar in heavy large nonaluminum saucepan. Gradually blend in hot milk using wooden spoon. Place over medium-low heat and stir until foam disappears from surface and custard leaves path on back of spoon when finger is drawn across; do not boil. Remove from heat. Add salt and whisk until very foamy. Strain through fine sieve into large bowl. Add vanilla. Cool, then refrigerate 12 hours or overnight.

For strawberry sherbet: Puree 1 pound strawberries, jam, lemon juice and salt in blender until smooth. Strain through fine sieve. Pour into flat 1-quart container. Freeze until solid.

Transfer vanilla mixture to ice cream maker and process according to manufacturer's instructions.

Place sherbet in refrigerator to soften.

Spoon ³/₄-inch layer of vanilla ice cream into 6 balloon wine glasses. Add ³/₄-inch layer of strawberry sherbet, then top sherbet with another ³/₄-inch layer of ice cream. Cover with plastic wrap. Freeze until ready to serve.

Puree whole strawberries; strain. Mix with sliced berries in medium bowl. Blend in vinegar and powdered sugar to taste. Cover sauce and refrigerate.

Spoon sauce over coupes. Garnish with mint or basil leaves and serve.

La Mystère

This dessert is found in one guise or another on the menu of many bistros.

6 servings

- 2 8³/₄-ounce cans chestnut spread (crème de marrons)*
- 2 ounces unsweetened chocolate, coarsely chopped
- ¹/₄ cup (¹/₂ stick) unsalted butter, chopped
- 4 to 6 tablespoons whipping cream

- 1 quart rich vanilla ice cream
- ³/₄ cup whipping cream, whipped with ¹/₄ teaspoon vanilla
- ¹/₂ cup sliced almonds, toasted
- 6 glacéed chestnuts*

Stir chestnut spread, chocolate and butter in top of double boiler set over hot (not boiling) water until mixture is smooth. Stir in enough cream to make thick sauce. (*Can be prepared 3 days ahead and refrigerated.*)

Before serving, remelt sauce over very low heat, stirring frequently. Place 2 scoops ice cream into dessert dishes. Spoon about ¹/₄ cup sauce over each. Top with whipped cream, almonds and glacéed chestnut and serve.

*Available at specialty foods stores and in some supermarkets.

Chocolate Truffle Bombe with Hazelnuts

8 servings

3 cups half and half
1 cup superfine sugar
7 egg yolks, room temperature

¾ cup unsweetened cocoa powder

⅔ cup whipping cream
6 ounces bittersweet or semisweet
   chocolate

¼ cup praline liqueur or Frangelico
¼ cup coarsely chopped husked
   toasted hazelnuts
1 tablespoon Grand Marnier

Chocolate curls (optional)

Cook half and half and sugar in heavy medium saucepan over low heat until sugar dissolves, swirling pan occasionally. Increase heat and bring to boil. Let cool 5 minutes. Whisk mixture into yolks. Return to saucepan. Stir over medium heat using wooden spoon until mixture registers 175°F on candy thermometer, about 8 minutes.

Sift cocoa powder into large bowl of electric mixer. Beat in hot custard at medium speed until cocoa dissolves. Cool, then refrigerate until thoroughly chilled, preferably overnight.

Pour chilled custard into ice cream maker and process according to manufacturer's instructions. Transfer to bowl and freeze until ice cream is firm enough to shape without melting.

Meanwhile, bring cream to boil. Remove from heat. Add chocolate and stir until melted. Blend in liqueur, hazelnuts and Grand Marnier. Cool truffle mixture to room temperature.

Line bottom of 5-cup ring mold with ¾ of ice cream (reserve remainder for top). Using fingers or small spoon, push ice cream up sides of mold, leaving deep groove in center (freeze several minutes to firm if necessary). Pour truffle mixture into groove. Spread remaining ice cream over top. Cover with foil and freeze at least 3 hours. (*Can be prepared several days ahead.*)

Run sharp knife around inside and outside edges of mold to loosen. Dip mold briefly into very hot water. Unmold onto platter. Wipe away any melted chocolate. Smooth outside surface with thin steel spatula. Return to freezer. To serve, let bombe stand in refrigerator until slightly softened (time will vary depending on how long bombe is frozen). Garnish center of bombe with chocolate curls if desired.

Cakes and Tortes

Pear Cake Savoyarde

8 to 10 servings

10 tablespoons (1¼ sticks) unsalted
    butter, room temperature
⅔ cup sugar
3 tablespoons fresh lemon juice
3 tablespoons dark rum
4 to 5 semi-ripe Bosc pears

½ cup sugar
1 teaspoon finely grated lemon peel
⅓ teaspoon salt
2 eggs
1 cup plus 2 tablespoons all purpose
   flour sifted with 1 teaspoon
   baking powder

Preheat oven to 375°F. Grease 10-inch deep-dish glass pie plate with 1½ table-spoons butter. Sprinkle bottom with ⅔ cup sugar, lemon juice and 2 tablespoons rum. Peel pears, halve lengthwise and core. Cut halves crosswise into ¼-inch slices; flatten slightly with palm of hand. Arrange slices round side down in concentric circles in prepared plate. Bake until pears are lightly caramelized and very tender, about 1 hour. Cool pears slightly. Reduce oven temperature to 350°F.

Cream remaining 8½ tablespoons butter in bowl of electric mixer. Blend in remaining ½ cup sugar, 1 tablespoon rum, lemon peel and salt and mix until smooth. Beat in eggs 1 at a time. Fold in flour. Spoon mixture evenly over pears. Bake until skewer inserted in center of cake comes out clean, 25 to 30 minutes. Immediately invert cake onto platter. Spread any caramel remaining in pie plate over pears. Serve at room temperature.

Applejack Cake Filled with Candied Apples

6 to 8 servings

Génoise
- 1 tablespoon butter
- 1 tablespoon all purpose flour
- 4 eggs, room temperature
- ½ cup sugar
- ⅓ cup applejack
- Pinch of salt
- 1 cup all purpose flour
- ¼ cup (½ stick) unsalted butter, melted

Candied Apples
- 2 tablespoons (¼ stick) butter
- 12 medium-size Granny Smith apples (about 4½ pounds total), peeled, quartered and cored
- ⅔ cup sugar
- ¼ cup apple cider
- 8 tablespoons applejack

- 1½ cups whipping cream
- 3 tablespoons powdered sugar
- ⅔ cup sliced almonds, toasted

For génoise: Preheat oven to 325°F. Grease and flour 8-inch square cake pan with 1 tablespoon each butter and flour. Beat eggs and sugar in large bowl of electric mixer until slowly dissolving ribbon forms when beaters are lifted, 5 minutes. Beat in applejack and salt until ribbon forms again and mixture almost forms peaks, about 4 minutes. Gently fold in flour and then melted butter. Turn into prepared pan. Bake until sides shrink slightly from pan, about 35 minutes. Invert onto rack and cool completely.

For apples: Preheat oven to 375°F. Coat 1 large glass baking dish or 2 medium dishes with 2 tablespoons butter. Arrange apples in dish(es) rounded side up. Sprinkle with ⅔ cup sugar. Bake until apples turn deep golden brown, about 1 hour. Transfer apples to buttered plate. Add cider and 4 tablespoons applejack to baking dish, scraping to dissolve all caramelized sugar. Pour into small heavy saucepan and boil syrup until reduced to 3 tablespoons. Brush over apples. Let mixture cool completely.

To assemble, cut ⅓-inch layer from top of cake using long serrated knife and set aside. Form cake into box by cutting out center using grapefruit knife, leaving ⅓- to ½-inch-thick sides and bottom. Lightly brush interior of cake with 1½ tablespoons applejack.

Whip cream with 2 tablespoons applejack and powdered sugar until soft peaks form. Spread ¼-inch layer of cream around inside of cake. Arrange all but 12 apple quarters in cake, packing tightly. Cover with ¼ inch cream. Place top layer on cake. Brush with remaining ½ tablespoon applejack. Spread cream on sides and top of cake. Gently press almonds into sides. Arrange 3 apple quarters decoratively on each corner of cake. Refrigerate cake until ready to serve.

Traditional Rum Babas

These small cakes are baked in special baba molds, but sixteen 2½- to 3-inch muffin cups can be used instead. Spoon 2 tablespoons dough into each. Bake for about 12 minutes.

Makes 12

⅔ cup dark raisins
1 tablespoon golden rum

Basic Baba Dough*

Basic Baba Syrup**

7 to 9 tablespoons golden rum

1 cup apricot preserves
2 tablespoons water
6 candied cherries, halved
24 almond slices

Rinse raisins under water; drain. Place in small jar. Add 1 tablespoon rum. Cover and shake. Let stand 1 hour.

Generously butter twelve ½-cup baba or dariole molds. Drain raisins, then fold into dough using wooden spoon. Spoon 3 tablespoons dough into each mold. Arrange on baking sheet, spacing 2 inches apart. Cover with plastic. Let dough rise in warm area 25 minutes. Remove plastic and let dough rise to top of molds, 15 to 30 minutes.

Position rack in center of oven and preheat to 400°F. Transfer baking sheet to oven and bake babas until tester inserted in centers comes out clean, 15 minutes. Unmold babas onto rack. Cool completely.

Place 1 baba, rounded side down, in hot syrup in saucepan. Let stand 5 seconds. Ladle syrup over baba until cake is uniformly moist and softened but not soggy, rolling baba in pan. Using slotted spoon, arrange baba on side on rack set over tray. Repeat with remaining babas, reheating syrup occasionally. Slowly spoon any remaining syrup over babas. Let stand 30 minutes.

Arrange babas on sides on large plate. Slowly spoon 1 teaspoon rum over each, rolling baba. Spoon ½ to 1 teaspoon more rum over each.

Arrange babas on sides on rack. Melt preserves with water in heavy small saucepan over low heat. Strain glaze, pressing to extract as much liquid as possible. Return to saucepan and reheat until beginning to bubble. Mix in 1 tablespoon rum. Brush glaze on all sides of babas. Arrange babas on sides on platter. Decorate each with candied cherry half and 2 almond slices. Brush cherries lightly with glaze. Cool 10 minutes. (*Can be prepared 2 days ahead. Cover tightly and refrigerate.*) Serve babas at room temperature.

---

*Basic Baba Dough

12 to 16 servings

1 envelope dry yeast
1 teaspoon sugar
¼ cup warm water (105°F to 115°F)

2 cups unbleached all purpose flour
4 eggs, room temperature

1 tablespoon sugar
1 teaspoon salt
7 tablespoons unsalted butter, cut into 14 pieces

Sprinkle yeast and 1 teaspoon sugar over water; stir to dissolve. Let stand until foamy, about 10 minutes.

Hand Method

Sift flour into large bowl and make well in center. Add 2 eggs, 1 tablespoon sugar and salt to well and blend with wooden spoon, gradually drawing 2 to 3 tablespoons flour from inner edge of well into center. Add remaining 2 eggs and yeast mixture to well. Stir until soft, sticky dough forms. Using cupped hand, slap dough against bowl for 1 minute. Transfer to lightly oiled bowl. Arrange butter pieces side by side atop dough. Cover bowl with plastic. Let dough rise in warm area until doubled, about 1 hour.

Fold butter into dough using wooden spoon. Gently slap dough against bowl until butter is blended in completely.

Processor Method

Process yeast mixture, eggs and 1 tablespoon sugar until well blended, about 5 seconds. Sift in flour and salt and mix until smooth, 30 seconds. (If dough is not smooth, transfer to bowl and slap against bowl until smooth.) Transfer to lightly oiled bowl. Arrange butter pieces side by side atop dough. Cover bowl with plastic wrap. Let dough rise in warm area until doubled, about 1 hour.

Fold butter into dough using wooden spoon. Gently slap dough against bowl until butter is blended in completely.

**Basic Baba Syrup

Makes about 2¹/₂ cups

2 cups water
1¹/₄ cups sugar

Cook water and sugar in heavy medium saucepan over low heat, swirling pan occasionally, until sugar dissolves completely. Increase heat and bring to boil. Remove syrup from heat.

Individual Nut Meringue Cakes with Chocolate Whipped Cream

8 servings

16 individual hazelnut-almond meringues (see page 114 for Basic Nut Meringues and Variations)
3 ounces semisweet chocolate, finely chopped

1 cup well-chilled whipping cream
2 teaspoons sugar
1 teaspoon vanilla
  Powdered sugar (optional)

Trim edges of meringues to even if necessary. Melt chocolate in double boiler over barely simmering water; stir until smooth. Remove from heat. Whip cream with sugar and vanilla in large bowl until stiff peaks form. Remove chocolate from over water. Cool 30 seconds. Quickly stir in half of whipped cream. Fold chocolate mixture into remaining whipped cream. Transfer filling to pastry bag fitted with medium star tip.* Pipe filling around top edge of flat side of 1 meringue, then fill in center in spiral pattern. Pipe second layer of filling atop first. Gently set flat surface of second meringue on filling to form sandwich; do not smooth sides. Transfer to tray. Repeat with remaining meringues and filling. Cover and refrigerate until set, at least 3 hours. (*Can be prepared 8 hours ahead.*) Just before serving, sift powdered sugar over tops of cakes.

*Filling can also be spread. Gently layer ¹/₄ cup filling evenly over flat side of 1 meringue. Set flat surface of second meringue on filling to form sandwich; smooth sides.

Basic Nut Meringues

Sandwich these airy, crunchy layers with rich buttercream, mousse or ice cream to create an elegant gâteau. Or simply pair them with whipped cream and fruit for a simple light dessert.

Makes two 8-inch rounds

³/₄ **to 1 cup nuts (see Variations)**
¹/₂ **cup plus 8 teaspoons sugar**
  1 **tablespoon cornstarch**

4 **egg whites, room temperature**
¹/₈ **teaspoon cream of tartar**

Position rack in center of oven and preheat to 300°F. Butter 2 nonstick baking sheets and dust with flour. Or, lightly butter corners of 2 baking sheets; line with parchment paper or foil. Butter parchment or foil; dust with flour. Trace 8-inch circle onto each prepared sheet, using 8-inch springform pan rim as guide.

Finely grind nuts with ¹/₂ cup sugar in processor, 15 to 30 seconds, stopping occasionally to scrape down sides of work bowl. Transfer to medium bowl. Sift cornstarch over; stir with fork to blend. Using electric mixer, beat whites with cream of tartar in large bowl until soft peaks form, beginning at medium speed and gradually increasing to medium-high speed. Increase speed to high; gradually add remaining 8 teaspoons sugar and beat until stiff and shiny but not dry. Sprinkle ¹/₃ of nut mixture over whites and fold gently until just combined. Repeat with remaining nut mixture. Immediately spoon meringue into pastry bag fitted with ¹/₂-inch plain tip. Pipe meringue over each circle on prepared sheets in spiral pattern, starting in center and covering completely.

Bake 30 minutes. (If meringues do not fit on 1 rack, position 1 rack in upper third of oven and 1 in lower third. Switch positions after 15 minutes.) Reduce temperature to 275°F. Continue baking meringues until light brown and dry, about 15 minutes; meringues will firm as they cool. Using large metal spatula, gently release meringues from baking sheets. If sticky on bottom, bake 5 more minutes. Transfer to rack and cool completely. Store in airtight container. (*Nut meringues can be prepared 5 days ahead and stored at room temperature or 1 month ahead and frozen.*)

Variations

Almond: Use ³/₄ cup (about 4 ounces) blanched almonds.

Hazelnut: Use 1 cup (about 4 ounces). Toast hazelnuts in shallow baking pan in 350°F oven 8 minutes. Transfer to strainer. Rub hazelnuts against strainer with kitchen towel to remove skins. Cool completely.

Hazelnut-almond: Use ¹/₂ cup (about 2 ounces) hazelnuts and ¹/₃ cup (about 1³/₄ ounces) unblanched almonds. Place nuts in separate baking pans; toast in 350°F oven 8 minutes. Husk hazelnuts as above. Cool completely.

Pecan: Use 1 cup (about 3³/₄ ounces).

Walnut: Use 1 cup (about 3¹/₂ ounces).

Macadamia nut: Use 1 cup (about 4¹/₂ ounces) unsalted macadamia nuts.

Pistachio: Use 1 cup (about 4¹/₂ ounces) shelled unsalted pistachios or use 8 ounces unshelled pistachios.

Individual nut meringues: Trace sixteen 3-inch circles on prepared sheets, using cookie cutter or beverage glass as guide and spacing ¹/₂ inch apart. Pipe meringue over circles as above. Bake in 300°F oven 30 minutes. Reduce temperature to 275°F. Continue baking until light brown and dry, about 10 minutes.

❧ Index

Alsatian Ham-stuffed Kugelhopf
  with Chervil and Mustard Sauce,
  57
Alsatian Style Chicken Sautéed in
  Beer, 63
Anchoiade, 26
Appetizers and First Courses, 2–16
  Basil Sausage in Saffron Brioche, 5
  Beet Salad with Marinated Turnip
    Slices, 28
  Brandade of Salt Cod on Garlic
    Croutons, 8
  Cabbage Salad with Tuna, 30
  Clams Steamed in Wine Broth, 6
  Goat Cheese Butter, Herbed, 2
  Goat Cheese, Marinated, 2
  Jambon Persillé, 12
  Leek and Ham Timbales, 11
  Lobster, Oyster and Zucchini
    Tartlets in Champagne Sauce, 3
  Mussel Salad, Warm, with Shallot
    Dressing, 29
  Oysters Baked with Rouille, 7
  Oysters in Cider Vinegar Butter, 6
  Pâté, Duck, with Walnuts, 14
  Pâté, Herbed Chicken, 13
  Prawns, Tiger, Provençal, 7
  Scallop and Watercress Salad, 29
  Snails in Puff Pastry Shells, 4
  Sole and Scallop Pâté with
    Smoked Salmon and Sorrel, 9
  Tarts, Cherry Tomato and
    Gruyère, 2
  Terrine, Game, Chef's, 15
  Terrine, Veal, 14
  Trout Mousse with Mushroom
    Sauce, 10
  Wild Mushroom Salad, 28
Apple
  Clafouti à la Ritz, 100

and Root Vegetable Soup, 18
Sauce Fritters, 103
Applejack Cake Filled with Candied
  Apples, 111
Artichoke and Cauliflower Gratin,
  86
Asparagus, Baked Eggs with, 38
Asparagus and Candied Onions, Pot-
  roasted Chicken with, 65

Baba Dough, Basic, 112; Baba Syrup,
  Basic, 113
Bachelor's Confiture, 97
Bacon-Onion Baked Eggs, 38
Baguettes, Gruyère, 89
Basil Sausage in Saffron Brioche, 5
Bean Soup, Two, 19
Beans. See Green Beans, White
  Beans
Beef, 46–48
  Boeuf à la Ficelle with Marrow,
    Mustard and Shallot Butter, 46
  Roast, with Sweet Red Pepper and
    Zucchini Relish, 47
  Stew and Vegetables with Red
    Wine, 48
Beet Salad with Marinated Turnip
  Slices, 28
Belgian Endive, Ham and Cheese
  Gratin, 85
Beurre Blanc, 9
Bombe, Chocolate Truffle with
  Hazelnuts, 110
Brandade of Salt Cod on Garlic
  Croutons, 8
Bread(s), 87–94. See also Brioche,
  Rolls
  Chestnut and Dried Pear, 94
  French Custard Toast, 42
  Gruyère Baguettes, 89

Gruyère-Walnut Loaf, 93
Hearth, 87
Pain Ordinaire, 88; Variations, 89
Pepper Seed Thin, 90
and Vegetable Soup, Rich, 22
Walnut, 93
Brioche. See also Rolls
  with Caramelized Almond
    Topping, Rich, 91
  Glazed Currant, 92
  Saffron, Basil Sausage in, 5
Brittany
  Fish Soup, 27
  -style, Grilled Red Snapper Saint-
    Malo, 74
  Style Shortbread, 104
Broccoli, Crunchy, Gratin, 86
Burgundy-style Jambon Persillé, 12
Burgundy-style Omelets with Bacon
  and Mushrooms, 39
Butter
  Cider Vinegar, Oysters in, 6
  Herbed Goat Cheese, 2
  Whipped Honey, 93

Cabbage and Apples, Sautéed,
  Smoked Garlic Sausage with, 60
Cabbage Salad with Tuna, 30
Cake(s)
  Applejack Filled with Candied
    Apples, 111
  Nut Meringues, Basic, 114;
    Variations, 114
  Nut Meringues with Chocolate
    Whipped Cream, Individual,
    113
  Pear Savoyarde, 110
  Rum Babas, Traditional, 112
Candied Apples, 111
Caramelized Fig Tart, 101

Carrot(s)
and Fennel, Wild Rice Pilaf with, 87
Pea and Salsify Sauté, 83
and Tomato Soup, Creamy, 23
Cauliflower and Artichoke Gratin, 86
Cauliflower Soup with Cinnamon, 19
Chanterelle Hazelnut Soup, 21
Chard-Morel Filling, Veal Rolls with, 50
Cheese Dishes, 40–44. See also Name of Cheese
Cheeses, French, Glossary of, 40–41
Chef's Game Terrine, 15
Cherry Tomato. See Tomato
Chervil and Mustard Sauce, 58
Chestnut(s)
and Dried Pear Bread, 94
Mushrooms and Onions, Pork Chops Baked with, 56
Pork with, Farm-style, 57
Chèvre. See Goat Cheese
Chicken, 62–66
Braised with Triple Onions, 64
Coq au Vin, 63
Fricassée, Legs in Gamay, 66
Niçoise Style, 65
Pâté, Herbed, 13
Pot-roasted with Candied Onions and Asparagus, 65
Roast with Garlic Croutons, 62
Roast with Wild Mushrooms, 62
Salad, Sweet and Sour, 32
Sautéed in Beer Alsatian Style, 63
Stock, Quick, 12
Chocolate
Soufflé, 108
Truffle Bombe with Hazelnuts, 110
Truffles, Savoie-style, 105
Clafouti, Apple, à la Ritz, 100
Clams Steamed in Wine Broth, 6
Cod. See Red Snapper, Salt Cod
Coffee Soufflé, 108
Cognac Crème Anglaise, 106
Confiture, Bachelor's, 97
Cookies. See also Truffles
Madeleines, Spiced, 104
Shortbread, Brittany Style, 104
Coq au Vin, 63
Corn, Mussel Soup with, 24
Cornish Hens Braised with Apple, Potato and Turnip Stuffing, 67
Country-style Rye Rolls, 90
Coupes Plougastel, 109
Cream Cheese with Pear and Cider Butter, 99
Cream Sauce, 85

Crème Anglaise, Cognac, 106
Crème Fraîche, 20
Crepes, Buckwheat, Sausages Wrapped in, 59
Croutons, Garlic, 31, 62
Cucumbers, Mustard-glazed, 75
Custard, Flagnarde, 105

Dessert, 96–110. See also Cake, Tart
Apple Clafouti à la Ritz, 100
Apple Sauce Fritters, 103
Chocolate Truffle Bombe with Hazelnuts, 110
Coupes Plougastel, 109
Cream Cheese with Pear and Cider Butter, 99
Crème Anglaise, Cognac, 106
Flagnarde, 105
Fruit, Dried, Ragout of, 96
Fruit Salad with Bachelor's Confiture, 96
Fruit, Wine- and Ginger-marinated, 96
La Mystère, 109
Peach Mousse, Soft, with Raspberry Sauce and Fresh Currants, 108
Prune Turnovers, Little, 97
Rice Pudding, Rich, with Poached Pears and Marmalade Sauce, 106
Soufflé, Basic Sweet, 107; Variations, 108
Strawberry Delights, 98
Dressing, Sun-dried Tomato, 36
Duck
Fillets, Grilled with Juniper Berries, 68
Leg, Radish and Zucchini Ragout, 69
Pâté with Walnuts, 14
and Potato Salad, 33
Stock, 69

Eggplant Gratin, Easy, 86
Eggplant and Parmesan Soufflé, 42
Eggs
Bacon-Onion, Baked, 38
Baked with Asparagus, 38
Omelets, Burgundy-style, with Bacon and Mushrooms, 39
Endive. See also Belgian Endive
Curly, Salad with Garlic Croutons, 31
Escarole Salad with Bacon, Vegetables and Fried Onions, 30

Fennel and Carrots, Wild Rice Pilaf with, 87
Fennel Soup with Crème Fraîche and

Bacon Lardons, 20
Fig Tart, Caramelized, 101
First Courses. See Appetizers and First Courses
Fish, 74–78. See also Name of Fish
Fumet, 80
Soup, Brittany, 27
Soup, Niçoise, with Anchoiade and Rouille, 25
Steamed with Hard Cider, Apples and Celery Root, 78
Stock, 26
Flagnarde, 105
Four-Onion Soup, 21
French Cheeses, Glossary of, 40–41
French Custard Toast (Pain Perdu), 42
Fricassée of Chicken Legs in Gamay, 66
Fritters, Apple Sauce, 103
Fruit(s). See also Name of Fruit
Ragout of Dried, 96
Salad with Bachelor's Confiture, 96
Wine- and Ginger-marinated, 96

Game and Pistachio Sausages, 70
Game Terrine, Chef's, 15
Garlic
Croutons, 31, 62
and Fresh Tomato Sauce, 13
Soup, 18
Goat Cheese
Butter, Herbed, 2
Marinated, 2
Spinach Chèvre Walnut Tart, 44
Tart, 43
Veal Chops Stuffed with Chèvre and Dill, Sautéed, 50
Gratin
Leek and Swiss Chard, 40
of Turnips, Pork Tenderloin Sauté with, 55
Vegetable, 84; Variations, 85
Green Beans and Tomato Salad, Vodka- marinated, 32
Green Beans in Walnut Oil, Warm, 82
Green Herb Soup with Polenta Garnish, 23
Green Salad, Mixed with Goat Cheese and Mustard Vinaigrette, 32
Gruyère
Baguettes, 89
and Cherry Tomato Tarts, 2
-Walnut Loaf, 93

Ham
Jambon Persillé, 12

and Leek Timbales, 11
Steaks, Grilled with Onions and
    Raisins, 58
-stuffed Kugelhopf with Chervil
    and Mustard Sauce, 57
Hazelnut Chanterelle Soup, 21
Hearth Bread, 87
Herb Soup, Green with Polenta
    Garnish, 23
Herbed Chicken Pâté, 13
Herbed Goat Cheese Butter, 2
Honey Butter, Whipped, 93

Jambon Persillé, 12

Kugelhopf, Ham-stuffed, with
    Chervil and Mustard Sauce, 57

Lamb, 53–54
    Breast of, Stuffed, 54
    Loin of, with Red Wine, Onion
        and Rosemary, 53
    Roast, Marinated, 53
    Sausage and White Bean Salad,
        Warm, 34
    Stock, Rich, 54
Leek
    and Butternut Squash Soup,
        Cream of, 22
    Crookneck Squash and Watercress
        Soup, 22
    and Ham Timbales, 11
    and Mushroom Gratin, 85
    and Swiss Chard Gratin, 40
Lemon Soufflé, 108
Lettuce and Wilted Spinach Salad,
    31
Lobster, Oyster and Zucchini
    Tartlets in Champagne Sauce, 3

Madeleines, Spiced, 104
Marinated Goat Cheese, 2
Marinated Lamb Roast, 53
Mayonnaise, Mustard, 12
Mediterranean Potato Salad with
    Mussels and Shrimp, 35
Mediterranean Rice Pilaf, 86
Meringue Cakes, Individual Nut,
    with Chocolate Whipped Cream,
    113
Meringues, Nut, Basic, 114;
    Variations, 114
Morel-Chard Filling, Veal Rolls
    with, 50
Morels, Veal Scallops with, 49
Mousse, Soft Peach with Raspberry
    Sauce and Fresh Currants, 108
Mousse, Trout with Mushroom
    Sauce, 10
Mushroom. See also Wild

Mushroom and Leek Gratin, 85
    Sauce, Trout Mousse with, 10
Mussel
    Salad, Warm, with Shallot
        Dressing, 29
    and Shrimp, Mediterranean
        Potato Salad with, 35
    Soup with Corn, 24
Mustard
    and Chervil Sauce, 58
    -glazed Cucumbers, 75
    Mayonnaise, 12
    Sherry, 46
    Tomato, 6
La Mystère, 109

Niçoise Fish Soup with Anchoiade
    and Rouille, 25
Niçoise Style Chicken, 65
Noodles, Sole with, 76
Normandy Rabbit in Cider, 71
Nut Meringue Cakes with Chocolate
    Whipped Cream, Individual, 113
Nut Meringues, Basic, 114;
    Variations, 114

Omelets, Burgundy-style, with
    Bacon and Mushrooms, 39
Onion(s)
    Candied and Asparagus, Pot-
        roasted Chicken with, 65
    Caramelized, 64
    Rolls, 91
    Soup, Four, 21
    Triple, Chicken Braised with, 64
Orange Soufflé, 108
Oyster(s)
    Baked with Rouille, 7
    in Cider Vinegar Butter, 6
    Cream Soup, 24
    Lobster and Zucchini Tartlets in
        Champagne Sauce, 3

Pain Ordinaire, 88; Variations, 89
Pain Perdu (French Custard Toast),
    42
Parmesan and Eggplant Soufflé, 42
Pastry
    Crust, Butter, 100
    Pie Crust, Special, 43
    Shells, Puff, Snails in, 4
Pâté. See also Terrine
    Duck with Walnuts, 14
    Herbed Chicken, 13
    Sole and Scallop with Smoked
        Salmon and Sorrel, 9
Pea, Carrot and Salsify Sauté, 83
Peach Mousse, Soft, with
    Raspberry Sauce and Fresh
    Currants, 108

Peach Tart, Fresh, 101
Pear(s)
    Cake Savoyarde, 110
    and Cider Butter, Cream
        Cheese with, 99
    Poached and Marmalade Sauce,
        Rich Rice Pudding with, 106
Pepper. See Red Pepper
Pepper Seed Thin Breads, 90
Pie Crust, Special, 43
Pilaf, Mediterranean Rice, 86
Pilaf, Wild Rice with Carrots and
    Fennel, 87
Pistachio Sausages, Game and, 70
Pistou, Basil and Mint, Steamed
    Seafood with, 79
Pistou Sauce, Sea Bass with, 76
Plum Compote, Sugar Tart with, 102
Pork, 55–57. See also Ham, Sausage
    Chops Baked with Chestnuts,
        Mushrooms and Onions, 56
    Farm-style, with Chestnuts, 57
    Loin with Prunes, 56
    Tenderloin Sauté with Gratin of
        Turnips, 55
Potato
    and Duck Salad, 33
    Galette, 83
    Salad, Mediterranean, with
        Mussels and Shrimp, 35
Prawns. See also Shrimp Tiger,
    Provençal, 7
Prune Turnovers, Little, 97
Puff Pastry Shells, Snails in, 4

Quatre Epices, 60

Rabbit Chasseur Sauté, 72
Rabbit in Cider, Normandy, 71
Ragout. See also Beef Stew
    of Dried Fruits, 96
    Duck Leg, Radish and Zucchini,
        69
    Spring Vegetable, 84
Red Pepper, Sweet, and Zucchini
    Relish, 47
Red Snapper Saint-Malo, Grilled, 74
Relish, Sweet Red Pepper and
    Zucchini, 47
Rice. See also Wild Rice
    Pilaf, Mediterranean, 86
    Pudding, Rich, with Poached
        Pears and Marmalade Sauce,
        106
Roast. See Beef, Chicken
Rolls. See also Brioche
    Onion, 91
    Rye, Country-style, 90
Rouille, 26
Rouille, Baked Oysters with, 7

Rum Babas, Traditional, 112
Rutabaga Puree, 83
Rye Rolls, Country-style, 90

Salad, 28–36
  Beet with Marinated Turnip
    Slices, 28
  Chicken, Sweet and Sour, 32
  Dressing, Sun-dried Tomato, 36
  Duck and Potato, 33
  Endive, Curly, with Garlic
    Croutons, 31
  Escarole with Bacon, Vegetables
    and Fried Onions, 30
  Fruit with Bachelor's Confiture,
    96
  Mixed Green with Goat Cheese
    and Mustard Vinaigrette, 32
  Mussel, Warm, with Shallot
    Dressing, 29
  Potato, Mediterranean, with
    Mussels and Shrimp, 35
  Scallop and Watercress, 29
  Spinach, Wilted, and Lettuce, 31
  Two-Cabbage with Tuna, 30
  of Vodka-marinated Tomato and
    Green Beans, 32
  White Bean and Lamb Sausage,
    Warm, 34
  Wild Mushroom, 28
Salmon, Baked Fillet, with Mustard-
  glazed Cucumbers, 74
Salmon and Sorrel, Smoked, with
  Sole and Scallop Pâté, 9
Salsify, Carrot and Pea Sauté, 83
Salt Cod, Brandade of, on Garlic
  Croutons, 8
Salt Cod and Vegetables in Herbed
  Tomato Sauce, 75
Sauce
  Anchoiade, 26
  Beurre Blanc, 9
  Chervil and Mustard, 58
  Cream, 85
  Crème Anglaise, Cognac, 106
  Mushroom, 10
  Mustard Mayonnaise, 12
  Pistou, 76
  Rouille, 7, 26
  Sherry Mustard, 46
  Tomato, Fresh, 42, 85
  Tomato and Garlic, Fresh, 13
  Tomato Mustard, 6
  Vinegar, 47
Sausage(s)
  Basil in Saffron Brioche, 5
  Game and Pistachio, 70
  Lamb, 35
  Smoked Garlic, Cabbage and

Apples Sautéed with, 60
  -stuffed Squabs with Apples and
    Calvados, 68
  Wrapped in Buckwheat Crepes, 59
Savoie-style Chocolate Truffles, 105
Savoyarde Pear Cake, 110
Scallop and Sole Pâté with Smoked
  Salmon and Sorrel, 9
Scallop and Watercress Salad, 29
Sea Bass with Pistou Sauce, 76
Seafood, 79–80. See also Name of
  Seafood
  Gratin, 79
  Seasoning, 78
  Steamed with Basil and Mint
    Pistou, 79
Sherry Mustard, 46
Shortbread, Brittany Style, 104
Shrimp. See also Prawns
  and Mussels, Mediterranean
    Potato Salad with, 35
Snails in Puff Pastry Shells, 4
Snapper. See Red Snapper
Sole with Noodles, 76
Sole and Scallop Pâté with Smoked
  Salmon and Sorrel, 9
Soufflé(s)
  Eggplant and Parmesan, 42
  Sweet, About, 107
  Sweet, Basic, 107; Variations, 108
Soup, 18–27
  Apple and Root Vegetable, 18
  Cauliflower with Cinnamon, 19
  Chanterelle Hazelnut, 21
  Fennel with Crème Fraîche and
    Bacon Lardons, 20
  Fish with Anchoiade and Rouille,
    Niçoise, 25
  Fish, Brittany, 27
  Four-Onion, 21
  Garlic, 18
  Green Herb with Polenta Garnish,
    23
  Mussel with Corn, 24
  Oyster Cream, 24
  Squash, Butternut,and Leek,
    Cream of, 22
  Squash, Crookneck, Leek and
    Watercress, 22
  Tomato and Carrot, Creamy, 23
  Two-Bean, 19
  Vegetable and Bread, Rich, 22
  Wild Mushroom, 20
Spiced Madeleines, 104
Spices, Mixed, Quatre Epices, 60
Spinach Chèvre Walnut Tart, 44
Spinach, Wilted, and Lettuce Salad,
  31
Spirits Soufflé, 108

Spring Vegetable Ragout, 84
Squabs, Sausage-stuffed with Apples
  and Calvados, 68
Squash, Butternut, and Leek Soup,
  Cream of, 22
Squash, Crookneck, Leek and
  Watercress Soup, 22
Stock
  Chicken, Quick, 12
  Duck, 69
  Fish, 26. See also Fish Fumet
  Lamb, Rich, 54
Strawberry Delights, 98
Sugar Tart with Plum Compote, 102
Sun-dried Tomato Dressing, 36
Sweet Soufflé. See Soufflé
Sweet and Sour Chicken Salad, 32
Swiss Chard
  with Bell Peppers, Gratin of, 85
  and Leek Gratin, 40
  -Morel filling, Veal Rolls with, 50

Tart(let)s
  Caramelized Fig, 101
  Cherry Tomato and Gruyère, 2
  Goat Cheese, 43
  Oyster, Lobster and Zucchini in
    Champagne Sauce, 3
  Peach, Fresh, 101
  Spinach Chèvre Walnut, 44
  Sugar with Plum Compote, 102
Terrine. See also Pâté
  Game, Chef's, 15
  Veal, 14
Tiger Prawns. See Prawns
Timbales, Leek and Ham, 11
Toast, French Custard, 42
Tomato
  and Carrot Soup, Creamy, 23
  Cherry, and Gruyère Tarts, 2
  Dressing, Sun-dried, 36
  and Garlic Sauce, Fresh, 13
  and Green Beans Salad, Vodka-
    marinated, 32
  Mustard, 6
  Sauce, Fresh, 42, 85
Trout Forestière, 77
Trout Mousse with Mushroom
  Sauce, 10
Truffle, Chocolate, Bombe with
  Hazelnuts, 110
Truffles, Chocolate, Savoie-style, 105
Tuna, Two-Cabbage Salad with, 30
Turbot with Lemon and Herbs, 77
Turnips, Gratin of, Pork Tenderloin
  Sauté with, 55
Turnovers, Little Prune, 97
Two-Bean Soup, 19
Two-Cabbage Salad with Tuna, 30

Veal, 49–52
Chops, Sautéed, Stuffed with
Chèvre and Dill, 50
Loin of, Roasted with Three
Vegetables, 51
Medallions of, Sautéed with
Garlic Cream Sauce, 49
Rolls with Chard-Morel Filling,
50
Scallops with Morels, 49
Terrine, 14
Vegetables, 82–86. *See also* Name of
Vegetable
and Beef Stew with Red Wine, 48
and Bread Soup, Rich, 22

Gratin, 84; Variations, 85
Ragout, Spring, 84
Root, and Apple Soup, 18
and Salt Cod in Herbed Tomato
Sauce, 75
Three, Roasted Loin of Veal with,
51
Vinegar Sauce, 47

Walnut Bread, 93
Walnut-Gruyère Loaf, 93
Watercress, Crookneck Squash and
Leek Soup, 22
Watercress and Scallop Salad, 29

White Bean and Lamb Sausage
Salad, Warm, 34
White Beans with Tomatoes and
Herbs, 82
Wild Mushroom(s). *See also*
Chanterelle, Morel
Roast Chicken with, 62
Salad, 28
Soup, 20
Wild Rice Pilaf with Carrots and
Fennel, 87
Wine- and Ginger-marinated Fruit,
96

Zuccini and Pearl Onion Gratin, 86

Credits and Acknowledgments

The following people contributed the recipes included in this book:

Ambassade d'Auvergne, Paris, France
Jean Anderson
Château d'Artigny, Montbazon, France
Sandre Cunha
Deirdre Davis
Harriet and Randy Derwingson
Helen Feingold
Flagons, New Orleans, Louisiana
Four Columns Inn, Newfane, Vermont,
Greg Parks, Chef
Cicero and Laurie Garner
Peggy Glass
Freddi Greenberg
Cathy and Don Hagen
Lyn Heller
Beth Hensperger
Jacki Horwitz
Hotel Cro-Magnon, Les Eyzies, France

Liisa Jasinski
Madeleine Kamman
Lynne Kasper
Jim Kronman
L'Arsenal, Strasbourg, France
Faye Levy
Susan Herrmann Loomis
Sheila Lukins
Abby Mandel
Linda Marino
Lydie Marshall
Michael McCarty
Carol McHarg
Jefferson and Jinx Morgan
Bruce Naftaly
Joanne O'Donnell
Pat and Steve Pepe
Sara Perry

Carole Rock
Betty Rosbottom
Julee Rosso
Michel Rostang
Jimmy Schmidt
Edena Sheldon
Jerry Slaby
André Soltner
Denise and Jerry St. Pierre
Michel Stroot
The Inn at Sawmill Farm, West Dover,
Vermont
Diane Ward
Anne Willan

Additional text was supplied by:
Faye Levy, *Sweet Soufflés;*
MaryJane Bescoby, *A Glossary of French Cheese.*

Special thanks to:

Editorial Staff:
  William J. Garry
  Barbara Fairchild
  Angeline Vogl
  MaryJane Bescoby

Graphics Staff:
  Bernard Rotondo
  Gloriane Harris

Rights and Permissions:
  Karen Legier

Indexer:
  Rose Grant

The Knapp Press
is a wholly owned subsidiary of
KNAPP COMMUNICATIONS CORPORATION

Composition by Andresen's Tucson Typographic Service, Inc., Tucson Arizona

This book is set in Sabon, a face designed by Jan Teischold in 1967
and based on early fonts engraved by Garamond and Granjon.